The Legend of AMDAHL

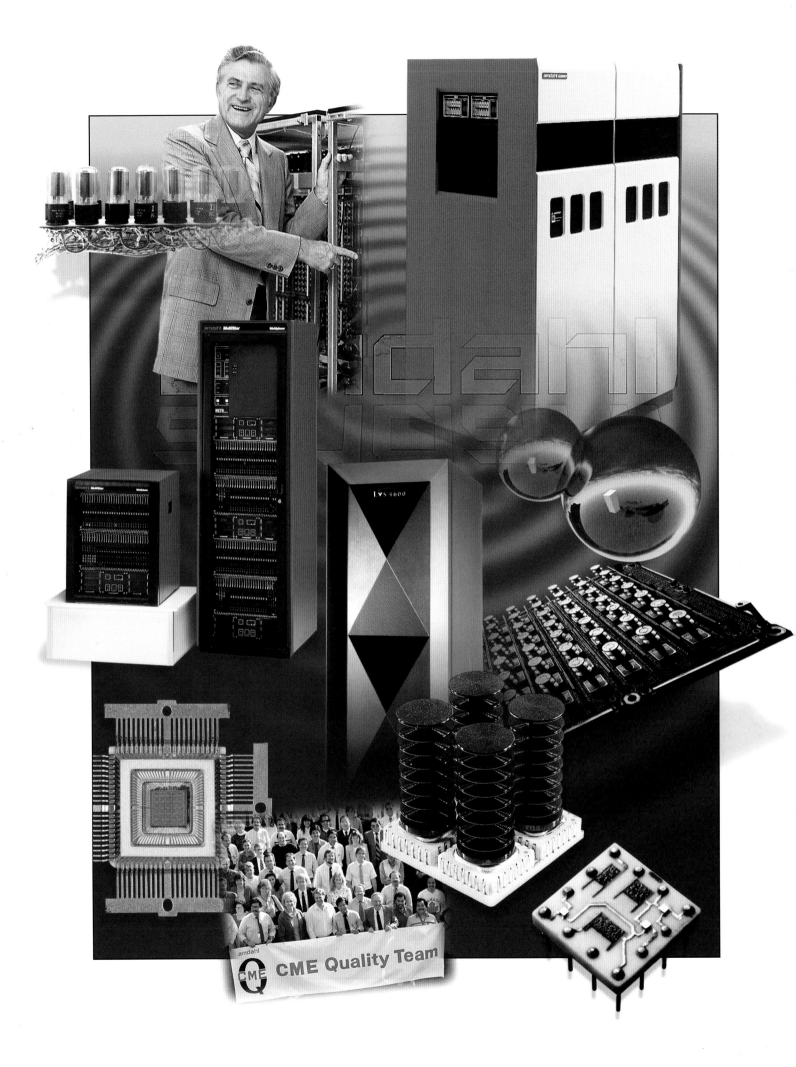

CME Quality Team

The Legend of AMDAHL

Jeffrey L. Rodengen

Edited by Jon VanZile
Design and layout by Jill Apolinario and Sandy Cruz

Also by Jeff Rodengen

The Legend of Chris-Craft

IRON FIST: The Lives
of Carl Kiekhaefer

Evinrude-Johnson and
The Legend of OMC

Serving the Silent Service:
The Legend of Electric Boat

The Legend of Dr Pepper/Seven-Up

The Legend of Honeywell

The Legend of Ingersoll-Rand

The Legend of Briggs & Stratton

The MicroAge Way

The Legend of Halliburton

The Legend of York International

The Legend of Stanley:
150 Years of The Stanley Works

The Legend of Nucor Corporation

The Legend of Goodyear:
The First 100 Years

The Legend of AMP

The Legend of Cessna

The Legend of VF Corporation

The Spirit of AMD

New Horizons:
The Story of Ashland Inc

The Legend of Rowan

The History of American Standard

The Legend of Mercury Marine

The Legend of Federal-Mogul

Against the Odds:
Inter-Tel—The First 30 Years

The Legend of Pfizer

State of the Heart: The Practical Guide
to Your Heart and Heart Surgery
with Larry W. Stephenson, M.D.

The Legend of Worthington Industries

The Legend of Trinity Industries

The Legend of IBP

The Legend of
Cornelius Vanderbilt Whitney

Publisher's Cataloging in Publication

Rodengen, Jeffrey L.
    The legend of Amdahl/Jeffrey L. Rodengen.
    p. cm.
    Includes bibliographical references and index.
    ISBN 0-945903-19-7

    1. Amdahl Corporation. 2. Computer industry—United States.
I. Title

HD9696.C64R64 1997   338.7'61004'0973
                            QBI97-40255

Write Stuff Syndicate, Inc.
1001 South Andrews Avenue, Second Floor • Fort Lauderdale, FL 33316
1-800-900-Book (1-800-900-2665) • (954) 462-6657
www.writestuffbooks.com

Library of Congress Catalog Card Number 96-60606
ISBN 0-945903-19-7

Completely produced in the United States of America
10 9 8 7 6 5 4 3 2 1

TABLE OF CONTENTS

Introduction		vi
Acknowledgments		viii
Chapter I	The Early Years	10
Chapter II	Development	18
Chapter III	The Launch	32
Chapter IV	Fighting Fear, Uncertainty and Doubt	40
Chapter V	Growth and Transition	50
Chapter VI	The Next Generation	58
Chapter VII	New Products and New Opportunities	74
Chapter VIII	Hitting the Mark	82
Chapter IX	A Time of Transition	92
Chapter X	Synergies	102
Chapter XI	The DMR and TRECOM Acquisitions	112
Chapter XII	Coming Full Circle	124
Notes to Sources		136
Index		141

INTRODUCTION

IN 1970, A BRILLIANT YOUNG ENGINEER left the world's largest computer manufacturer to start a small, underfinanced competitor. His name was Gene Amdahl, and he had been instrumental in helping develop the IBM 360 mainframe — the machine that introduced the world to the power of upgradable computing.

According to author Michael S. Malone, when Amdahl, who was by then one of IBM's top engineers, told his bosses he planned to found a mainframe competitor, the words "sounded insane. After all, in the previous 20 years, IBM had taken on the biggest firms in America and beaten them to their knees."

Yet Amdahl was determined that he could beat Big Blue at its own game. In 1970, he recruited a group of bright, ambitious engineers and on October 19 founded Amdahl Corporation. The company soon secured financing, including a significant investment from Japanese electronics giant Fujitsu, and the development process began on the first true mainframe competition to IBM.

Five years later, the Amdahl 470V/6 was ready for launch. This computer was a revolution in both the annals of business and the technology of computing. The group had designed a machine that was more powerful than the existing IBM 370/168, air cooled as opposed to the expensive water-cooled IBMs, and less expensive. It was also the first mainframe to incorporate LSI (large scale integrated) circuit technology.

The competition that followed between IBM, one of the world's largest corporations, and tiny Amdahl was fierce. Over the next years, the companies engaged in price wars and battled to introduce faster and more powerful mainframes.

Of course, the beneficiaries of this rivalry were consumers. Savvy customers soon learned that an Amdahl mug strategically placed on a desk during a sales call from the local IBM dealer could result in huge savings. Moreover, the competition held down the price of mainframe computing even while quality and speed increased rapidly. Amdahl Corporation, through sheer strength of will and brazen confidence in its mainframes, helped create the modern age of computing.

This alone is a lasting legacy and tribute to the company, but the story of the modern Amdahl Corporation is also a testament to corporate flexibility. The high-tech industry has never been kind to its participants. The pace of innovation increases exponentially, and new technologies appear that overnight can render entire segments of the industry obsolete.

Early on, Amdahl began to gird itself against the shifting fortunes of its industry. Only a few years after introducing its first machine, Amdahl began a diversification into communications systems and storage devices that would support its mainframe business. Amdahl CEO Jack Lewis declared that Amdahl would do anything necessary to serve the large-scale computing user.

Through the 1980s, this was enough. In 1987, Amdahl's yearly revenues surpassed $1 billion, driven mostly by mainframe, storage and communications hardware. Heading into the 1990s with yet another new mainframe, Amdahl was growing quickly. In 1990 it had registered more than $2 billion in annual revenues.

But there were forces moving behind this positive picture that did not bode well. Even as revenue skyrocketed, income was dropping. IBM had initiated another costly price war, and sales in Europe suddenly slowed. Worse for the mainframe market, however, was the rapid proliferation of the desktop computer. Instead of relying solely on mainframes, companies began building networks of personal computers that used a mainframe as the server. Because of the added power of so many smaller computers, the demand for mainframes dropped, and manufacturers found themselves in trouble. IBM, which for so long had been almost invincible, was forced to take one of the largest writedowns in business history as it coped with the new demands.

Amdahl, however, was better prepared. While the company was hit by the sudden shift, Amdahl was already in the midst of a fundamental transformation. No longer would it manufacture mainframes — in fact, in 1993, Amdahl struck an agreement with Fujitsu that the Japanese company would manufacture all of Amdahl's mainframes. Instead, Amdahl would change itself into a total solutions provider. "Wall Street wants to know whether Amdahl can change as the market requires," said company president and CEO Joe Zemke. "The answer is absolutely yes."

Once the decision had been made, announcements followed each other with alacrity. In 1993 and 1994, Amdahl entered into a series of alliances in an effort to move into consulting and professional services. Within a year, this new business represented 32 percent of revenues. In 1995,

Amdahl announced the acquisition of DMR Group, Inc., a Canadian professional services and consulting company. This was followed by the acquisition of TRECOM, another consulting and professional services organization. By 1996, a year of "sweeping change and significant progress," Amdahl had built one of the world's largest consulting and Year 2000 conversion businesses.

At the same time, longtime leader Joe Zemke retired and Jack Lewis, the former CEO, returned. Still reorganizing and assimilating the new companies, Amdahl found its income was dropping. Lewis began looking for a solution and soon found one with Fujitsu, Amdahl's oldest partner and one of its first investors.

In 1997, Amdahl was acquired by Fujitsu. Concurrently, Lewis announced his retirement and David Wright, executive vice president of the Amdahl Systems Group, was named CEO.

Under Wright, Amdahl has continued its evolution into one of the world's premier providers of complete solutions for large-scale information technology users. "Amdahl's goal, simply stated, is to be our customers' trusted, indispensable vendor of enterprise computing solutions," said Wright in 1998.

In 1998, its last year as a public company, Amdahl reported revenues of $2.1 billion. Of that, $1.4 billion came from software and professional services. The rest came from hardware and the company's new Millennium mainframe.

The story of Amdahl Corporation, beginning with the engineer who took on IBM and ending with a strategic transformation, represents an important chapter in the history of computing. Through its early machines, it made large-scale computing cost effective and faster. In later years, it became a global powerhouse of knowledge, helping companies better utilize the incredible power of computing. Throughout this sometimes riotous story, Amdahl's entrepreneurial, flexible spirit has remained intact.

"We set a precedent in the industry," Wright said. "As you go through the history of our company, we've changed ourselves in a number of ways. And change is good."

ACKNOWLEDGMENTS

A GREAT NUMBER OF PEOple assisted in the research, preparation and publication of *The Legend of Amdahl*.

The principal research was accomplished by my energetic and enterprising research assistant Kenneth Hartsoe.

This work would not have been possible without the generous cooperation of company leaders. David B. Wright, president and CEO, provided invaluable insight through hours of interviews. Likewise, company founder Gene Amdahl contributed his unique perspective to the early part of the story. The book benefited greatly from the kind cooperation of John "Jack" Lewis, former president and CEO, and chairman of the board; Joe Zemke, former president and CEO; and Eugene White, former president and CEO.

Thanks are also extended to Frank Carey, former chairman of IBM, for his interview.

Over the life of the project, the corporation communications staff provided invaluable guidance and suggestions regarding accuracy. Special thanks go to Bill Stewart, Douglas Gruehl, Christy Lang and Toni Dakan, each of whom took time from busy schedules to help.

Many Amdahl and Fujitsu executives, employees and retirees greatly enriched the book by discussing their experiences at the company. The author extends particular gratitude to these men and women for their candid recollections and anecdotes: Linda Alepin; David L. Anderson, former vice president and chief technology officer; Bruce Beebe, former senior vice president; Alan Bell, group president; Dave Brewer, former vice president; Allen Buskirk, former vice president; Ed Cardinal, who started with Amdahl in 1972; Frank Casagrande, TRECOM founding partner; Patrick Cashmore; Henry Cassel; John Cavalier; Dave Chambers, former vice president; Steve Coggins, former marketing director; Tony DeMory, former sales manager; Pierre Ducros, DMR founding partner; James Dutton, vice president; William F. Ferone, former vice president; Tom Fitzgerald; William Flanagan, group president; Chuck Fonner, former vice president, SmartCard Group; Joseph Francesconi, former vice president; Fred Gonzalez, associate general counsel; Glenn Grant; Greg Grodhaus, senior vice president; Greg Handschuh, vice president and general counsel; Yoshio Honda; Peter Labé, securities analyst; Reed W. Larsen, vice president; Robert Maier; John Matthews, a support technician during the first product launch; Wayne McIntyre, on the original sales team; Bill O'Connell, former senior vice president; Robert O'Neill, liaison between Amdahl and Fujitsu; John Palmer; Gene Plonka, a key financial figure; Michael Poehner, president and CEO, DMR Consulting Group; Anthony Pozos, senior vice president, human resources and corporate services; Charlie Pratt, vice president; Price Pritchett; Robert Sargenti, chief operating officer, DMR Consulting Group; Mike Shahbazian, vice president and treasurer; Harold O. Shattuck, former director of engineering; Edward Thompson, former vice president and chief financial officer; Ernest Thompson, former vice president and controller; Lyle Topham; Peter Williams; Kip Witter; and Yoshiro Yoskioka, board member and Fujitsu general manager.

As always, the author extends a special expression of thanks to the dedicated staff at Write Stuff Syndicate, Inc. Proofreader Bonnie Freeman and transcriptionist Mary Aaron worked quickly and efficiently. Indexer Erica Orloff assembled the comprehensive index. Particular thanks go to Jon VanZile, executive editor; Alex Lieber and Karen Nitkin, former editors; Melody Maysonet, senior editor; Heather Cohn and Marie Etzler, associate editors; senior art director Sandy Cruz; former art director Kyle Newton; Jill Apolinario and Rachelle Donley, art directors; Colleen Azcona and Amanda Fowler, assistants to the author; Marianne Roberts, office manager; Bonnie Bratton, director of marketing; Grace Kurotori, sales and promotions manager; Rafael Santiago, logistics specialist; and Karine Rodengen, project coordinator.

The Hollerith Tabulating Machine, invented by Herman Hollerith in 1890. Using the machine, operators tabulated the 1890 census in one-third the time of previous censuses. *(Photo courtesy of IBM archives.)*

CHAPTER ONE

THE EARLY YEARS
PRE-1970

"I'm really a glorified inventor."

— Gene Amdahl, 1996[1]

IN 1822, ENGLISH MATHMA-tician and engineer Charles Babbage earned the distinction of fathering the modern computer when he designed the Difference Machine. The novel device was a complicated steam-powered machine that could add, subtract, multiply and divide using directions that had been coded on cards. Babbage next envisioned the Analytical Machine, which combined mathematical functions and logic, opening the door for future calculations. The Analytical Machine was far beyond the technological capabilities of the time. Though it never got past the sketch-pad stage, Babbage's Analytical Machine formed the inspiration for many subsequent inventions.[2]

Decades later, Herman Hollerith of the United States Census Bureau introduced a punch-card system, making it possible to tabulate the 1890 census in one-third the time of past censuses. Hollerith founded the Automatic Tabulating Company and sold his technology to bankers, accountants, travel agents and other professionals who required large-scale recordkeeping. In 1924, Hollerith's company was acquired by Thomas J. Watson and renamed International Business Machines (IBM).

From 1939 to 1944, IBM funded research conducted at Harvard University for an electric calculating machine. After investing $1 million, IBM developed the Mark I, containing thousands of relays and nearly 500 miles of wire.

The ENIAC

For the most part, these devices remained obscured from the public eye. It wasn't until the introduction of the massive Electronic Numerical Integrator and Calculator (ENIAC) in 1946 that computing really caught people's imagination. This huge device was developed at the University of Pennsylvania with funding from the United States Army. The War Department needed to calculate trajectories for every possible combination of gun, shell and projectile. For this seemingly insurmountable task, John Mauchly and J. Presper Eckert of the University of Pennsylvania's Moore School of Engineering were contracted to develop the ENIAC. The ENIAC used vacuum tubes, which had no moving parts and were much faster than the mechanical switches used in the past.

The massive ENIAC was 100 feet long, 10 feet high and three feet deep. It used an astonishing 18,000 vacuum tubes. The tubes were so bright they attracted thousands of moths and generated so much heat that tubes were constantly blowing out. Teams of soldiers were dispatched to the swel-

A ceramic module used in the IBM 360 series, a revolutionary family of computers designed by Gene Amdahl. *(Photo courtesy of IBM archives.)*

IBM funded research at Harvard University to develop an electric calculating machine. After four years and $1 million, the Mark I was introduced in 1944. *(Photo courtesy of IBM archives.)*

1946 — Electronic Numerical Integrator and Calculator (ENIAC) is developed at the University of Pennsylvania.

1952 — Gene Amdahl is recruited by IBM.

1957 — IBM develops the 305 RAMAC (Random Access) computer.

tering room armed with peach baskets filled with replacement tubes.[3]

In the years following World War II, IBM continued to research and introduce various computing systems. During the 1950s, the company introduced the IBM 650, a 16-inch-long spinning drum that could magnetically hold 10,000 bits of memory on the 40 tracks inscribed around the drum. Memory at that time consisted of small round bits of magnetized iron oxide wired together like beadwork. These tiny spheres were magnetized clockwise or counterclockwise to contain memory.[4] An improvement to the use of these tiny cores was the IBM 305 RAMAC (Random Access) computer in 1957. It was the first system to utilize disks for memory storage. These 24-inch spinning disks stored 5 million characters and enabled an operator to retrieve data in less than a second.[5] Five years later, IBM improved on this technology, offering a system that allowed customers to remove disks and switch them for various file applications.[6]

IBM also marketed an early computer that reduced power consumption by 95 percent. This system relied on transistors, which were roughly

Generally thought of as the precursor to the modern mainframe, the Electronic Numerical Integrator and Calculator (ENIAC) used thousands of vacuum tubes, which generated tremendous amounts of light and heat. *(Photo courtesy of IBM archives.)*

1960 — IBM develops first production line for transistor assembly.

1967 — Amdahl formulates Amdahl's Law, an important theory in the field of parallel processing.

1964 — Amdahl is the principal architect of IBM's 360 family of computers.

1970 — Gene Amdahl leaves IBM to start his own company.

one two-hundredth the size of vacuum tubes and required only one percent of their power.[7]

In 1960, IBM engineers developed the nation's first high-production assembly line for transistors in Poughkeepsie, New York. The line could produce 1,800 transistors an hour, a necessary development since one mainframe computer in 1960 used more than 25,000 transistors.[8]

By the 1960s, engineers were steadily moving toward a more complex computing environment. Transistors represented a quantum leap from the temperamental vacuum tubes in terms of number and speed of instructions. The next step was system architecture, or the placement of transistors on a "chip" to make the signal path more efficient. As one IBM engineer pointed out in the late 1950s, "The key wasn't only the transistor card, it was the whole circuit packaging system — the back panel, the gate, the industrial design, the memories, the power supplies. Everything had to be standardized to assure high, predictable reliability, at reasonable cost, machine after machine after machine."[9] Customers wanted systems that were consistent, but the wide variety of mainframe units often caused confusion.[10]

To overcome this stumbling block in the growing mainframe industry, IBM in 1964 introduced the 360 line of mainframe computer systems, developed by engineer Gene Amdahl. The IBM 360 would

Above: The vacuum tubes in the ENIAC constantly needed replacement because overheating caused them to burn out. *(Photo courtesy of IBM archives.)*

Below: IBM introduced the 305 RAMAC system in 1957. *(Photo courtesy of IBM archives.)*

Inset: The key innovation of RAMAC was removable disks for memory storage. *(Photo courtesy of IBM archives.)*

become the most popular computer family of its day.

Gene Amdahl

Gene Amdahl was born in Flandreau, South Dakota, on November 16, 1922. He grew up on the family farm, attending school only when his chores on the homestead would allow. Even before the Great Depression, the Amdahl family was poor. Electric power didn't come to the farm until Gene was in high school. But even before electricity was a part of his life, Gene Amdahl loved to tinker. At age 12, he built a model of a helicopter rotor. He later built a crystal radio, only to discover that there were no radio stations within range.

After high school, Amdahl served in World War II, married Marian D. Quissell in 1946, then earned degrees in engineering and physics from South Dakota State University. He went on to earn a Ph.D. in theoretical physics at the University of Wisconsin. With the help of some professors, he designed a digital computer, which was then built by the university and called WISC (Wisconsin Integrally Synchronized Computer).

WISC's innovations beat IBM to the market.[11] WISC remained operational at the university until 1959, when the last man to maintain it took it home with him and used it as a backdrop for a pistol range. In later years, Amdahl acquired the bullet-riddled machine.

After IBM officials learned about WISC, they recruited Amdahl to work for them in 1952. Though he had no formal training in computer design, he exhibited a remarkable gift for problem-solving. "I work on the principle that there are a hundred ways to do anything," he said. "Just find them. I'm not really a scientist, although I am a theoretical physics doctor. I'm really a glorified inventor."[12]

Amdahl left IBM in 1955 to pursue other interests. At Ramo Woolridge in Los Angeles, he prepared several military and internal proposals in the data processing field. He also did the system planning for what became the RW440 process control computer. In 1956, Amdahl joined Aeronautics, a subsidiary of the Ford Motor Company, where he headed the commercial data processing department. He returned to IBM in 1960, working in Poughkeepsie, New York.

In 1963, Amdahl left New York to become a visiting professor at Stanford University in California. He liked the West Coast so much that he told IBM he planned to stay. Unwilling to lose one of their most valuable employees, executives at IBM created a job for him in California's Silicon Valley, at the company's research facility in Los Gatos.

A short while later, he was made an IBM Fellow, the highest research position at IBM. While he was on the phone receiving the exciting news, an earthquake rumbled through the region, making the floor shiver and the pictures on the wall clatter. Amdahl's knees felt weak as he literally felt the earth move. "I thought I was just being overwhelmed by an emotional reaction," he later recalled with a chuckle.[13]

In 1967, Amdahl formulated Amdahl's Law, a seminal theory in the field of parallel processing. Amdahl's Law made it possible to determine how much benefit additional processors would bring to a system. The greater the system's ability to process things at the same time (the more parallelizable it is), the greater the benefit. At the other extreme, a system that is not parallelizable at all would experience no benefit from additional processors because it would only be able to process one workload at a time. Since most systems have some functions that are parallelizable, Amdahl's law made it possible to determine the maximum "speedup" that could be achieved with more processors.

"It's based on nothing more than simple physics," Amdahl said. "It's a situation where you don't add speed, you add times. All I did was show that even if you can get a program or piece of a program to run at a hundred times its rate, because you are sharing it across a hundred processors, there are still tasks that you can't do that way. So I just figured out the maximum time for each of these programs and came out with a simple little algebraic formula that destroyed a lot of overly optimistic views."[14]

Amdahl's Law

$$speedup = \frac{1}{s + (1-s)/n} = mpl_{eff}$$

Amdahl's Law makes it possible to calculate the effective multiprocessing level of a work load, given the portion that can't be parallelized (s) and the number of processors (n).

The IBM 360

Amdahl was the lead designer of the revolutionary IBM 360 line of computers. It was the first family of computers that was standardized in terms of design, peripherals and software. All members of the 360 family ran on the standard FORTRAN and COBOL software languages and offered a unique system of computer time-sharing by being able to perform several operations at the same time. Most unique was its circuitry, which relied on small ceramic modules composed of diodes, transistors and solid-state circuits.[15] This Solid Logic Technology offered thousands of hours of operating time before failure.

The 360 immediately changed the computer market. For the first time, it was possible to upgrade and expand a computer system over time. A small company could buy a computer system, confident that as the company grew, it could add to the system without having to replace the software and peripheral equipment. More than 30,000 units of the 360 family of computers were sold to business, industry, universities and government facilities during the 1960s.[16] As a result, IBM virtually owned the market. Between 1964 and 1970, IBM commanded 70 percent of the mainframe computer market, with system users spending $200 million on application programming.[17] The 360, and the later 370, became the standard of the mainframe industry during the late 1960s.

However, IBM was something of a victim of its own success. Since software was much more expensive than the computers, consumers were resistant to any change that would force them to abandon their existing software. New systems would succeed only if they were compatible with the 360. Meanwhile, IBM had developed a pricing structure based exclusively on the amount of power a computer provided. Gene Amdahl thought that a more powerful computer could be manufactured at a more reasonable price, and he developed just such a system. But IBM wasn't interested. A faster, less expensive computer would only compete with the 360, and that was the last thing the computer giant wanted. Production costs for large systems were low compared to what customers were willing to pay for the machines. The company enjoyed large profits, confident that no competitor could penetrate its market dominance. Even a company with a superior product would have to convince consumers to abandon the tried-and-true IBM name and invest in a whole new software package.

But Amdahl was starting to think that the situation posed an opportunity for the right kind of company. The key would be to offer a computer that used IBM-compatible software and peripherals, while providing more power at a lower price.[18]

Meanwhile, his unhappiness at IBM was reaching a critical point. In 1970, IBM executives informed Amdahl that he could no longer serve on the board of directors of his brother's company, a consulting firm called Compata. "They thought it looked bad to have somebody on the board of another company in a computer field, even if the two companies weren't in competition," Amdahl recalled. He didn't have the heart to abandon his brother, especially during an economic recession. Although executives at IBM went to great lengths to persuade him to stay, Amdahl resigned. He left IBM in October 1970 and set out to start a company of his own.[19]

"He informed Big Blue that he planned to start a company to compete with the computer giant," wrote Michael S. Malone in *The Big Score*, a comprehensive look at Silicon Valley.

"They were brave words — and they also sounded insane. After all, in the previous 20 years, IBM had taken on the biggest firms in America and beaten them to their knees — and now this entrepreneurial upstart, with little prior management experience and no business experience, proposed to succeed where those heavyweights had failed."[20]

The IBM System 360 Model 40 was part of the popular 360 family of computers developed by Gene Amdahl. It was the first standardized family of computers in the industry, so customers could upgrade systems without replacing them. *(Photo courtesy of IBM archives.)*

Gene Amdahl's new company started to build facilities in the early seventies. Here, buildings A, E1 and M1 are shown among the empty fields that still dominated Sunnyvale at the time.

CHAPTER TWO
DEVELOPMENT
1970–1974

"A barrier to him was something that you just pushed to the side."

— Engineer Lyle Topham, describing Gene Amdahl[1]

GENE M. AMDAHL FOUNDED Amdahl Corporation on October 19, 1970. The company's stated goal was to "bring competition to the large-systems marketplace by providing quality processors that were compatible with the industry standard and offered a price-performance advantage to the user."[2] The industry standard, of course, was a direct reference to seemingly omnipotent IBM. Gene Amdahl's computer would run on IBM software, but it would be more powerful, smaller and less expensive than IBM's System 360 series. It was a brilliant strategy.

"A key piece of Gene's strategy was the belief that if one builds a machine that's cheap enough, relative to the IBM product, then IBM won't compete," said Harold O. Shattuck, a 1971 recruit from IBM who became director of engineering in 1973. "IBM won't give up its billions and billions in revenue to stop some little company doing a few tens of millions in business."[3]

Amdahl Corporation was cofounded by Raymond A. Williams, Jr., an experienced finance analyst from IBM who would serve as chief financial officer and a director during the company's first two years. He helped create a business plan and scrape together the capital needed to start the company before leaving in 1973.

Amdahl and Williams calculated they would need $33 million to $44 million in funding before the company would earn revenue.[4] With $33 million, the company would be able to develop and sell fewer than 100 machines. A $44 million investment would allow Amdahl to produce 150 machines.[5]

Their business plan required three phases of financing. An initial investment of $5 million would enable Amdahl to prove the circuit technology. A second investment of $12 million would be enough to create a demonstration system. Manufacturing and marketing the device would have to wait for the third phase of financing.

Amdahl knew it would be nearly impossible to convince investors to pour money into a start-up company that would battle IBM on its own turf. Too many others had tried and failed. To make matters worse, the economy was in the throes of a recession, and the capital gains tax had recently risen.[6]

Amdahl was also competing for funds with three other California computer companies — Mascor (Multiple Access Systems Corporation) in Cupertino, Gemini Computers in Orange County and Berkeley Computers in Berkeley.[7] The Heizer Corporation, a Chicago firm that helped distribute institutional funding, considered all four compa-

A chip carrier, this one shown without the heatsink, that would be used in Amdahl's first computer system, the 470V/6.

Gene Amdahl was able to secure funding to take on IBM because of his excellent reputation in the high-tech community.

nies before deciding that Amdahl's plan was the most viable. Heizer Corporation founder E.F. Heizer, Jr., saw that "this is a unique opportunity, and Amdahl is the one guy in the country who can carry it off."[8] Heizer's interest in IBM-compatible mainframes stemmed from his company's experience as a large shareholder of Control Data Corporation, a noncompatible mainframe manufacturer. "As they got bigger and bigger and tried to compete more and more, they found it tougher and tougher," he said.

"We didn't see anybody [except Amdahl] making a meaningful effort to compete with IBM on a compatible basis.... We thought we could help him from a business standpoint, and then he could help us from a technical standpoint. We considered it a pretty interesting combination of effort."[9]

Heizer originally offered $1 million, but Amdahl argued that his company couldn't even achieve its

October 19, 1970 — Amdahl Corporation is founded.

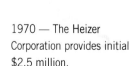

1970 — The Heizer Corporation provides initial $2.5 million.

1971 — Additional funding is provided by Fujitsu, Ltd.

first goal with that amount. Heizer, who would later serve on Amdahl Corporation's board of directors, reconsidered and agreed to invest $2.5 million. The decision was made shortly before Christmas of 1970.

With Heizer's decision to go with Amdahl Corporation, Mascor, Gemini Computers and Berkeley Computers closed due to a lack of needed financing. The collapse of these potential rivals allowed Amdahl Corporation to scoop up some of the brightest talent in the area. The company hired 22 people from Mascor, which had been working on a large time-sharing mainframe, and eight from the other two companies.[10] By the end of 1970, Amdahl had secured the initial investment he needed, hired an exceptional staff and started operations in a 6,000-square-foot facility at Kern Avenue and the Lawrence Expressway.[11]

"We Can Do Both"

One of Amdahl's goals was to create a much faster system. He wanted a cycle time of 8.33 nanoseconds, which was unheard of at the time. (A nanosecond is one-billionth of a second.)

Amdahl was undaunted, even though IBM's fastest machines were glacial in comparison, at 80 nanoseconds.[12] "A barrier to him was something that you just pushed to the side," said Lyle Topham, a mainframe developer recruited from Mascor.[13]

Amdahl didn't believe in compromise. "If you came to him and said, 'Look, Gene, we can do either this or this,' if you gave him a trade-off, he would say, 'If we really think about this and are smart about it, we can do both,'" said Dave Brewer, an engineer recruited from Mascor, who would retire in 1995 as vice president of special projects.

First impressions of Gene Amdahl could be misleading. His slow, deliberate speech and polite Midwestern manners didn't fit the profile of a computer whiz. A man with a pleasant face and piercing blue eyes, he would carry suitcases through airports for coworkers and take the time to chat with people at all levels of the company. "He had a way of putting you at ease while being very much up in the clouds," said Joe Francesconi, who left IBM in 1976 to become regional vice president for the Chicago area.[14] He later left Amdahl to become chief executive officer of N.E.T., or Network Equipment Technologies. Although Gene Amdahl

1971 — Fujitsu designers and engineers arrive at Amdahl Corporation to assist with the new system.

1973 — IBM announces that its new system will use virtual memory instead of real memory.

1973 — Study finds that 32 percent of large-scale computer users would consider switching to a new computer company.

1974 — Employees sign a petition saying they will leave if Gene Amdahl is replaced.

seemed more like a mild-mannered professor than a Silicon Valley entrepreneur, he was a legend among engineers.

Amdahl didn't seem to realize that he was smarter than most people. He would come up with an idea, scratch it out on the yellow pads he always used, and then expect engineers to turn it into a reality. But no matter how hard they worked, they often could not meet his expectations. For example, the system wound up with an initial cycle time of about 28 nanoseconds, almost 19 nanoseconds longer than what Amdahl had envisioned. "I'll give him the benefit of the doubt and say if you could clone him 50 times, you might have been able to do something close to 8⅓. But not us," said Brewer, who at the time was a development manager. "And besides, as we got further along in the project, cycle time turned out to be a lot less important than getting the machine out."[15]

A More Powerful Chip

Amdahl's computer would be the first to utilize large-scale integrated (LSI) circuitry. With LSI technology, many more components could be placed on each chip, providing more power at less cost. Amdahl tried to get several major companies to supply the circuitry, but Intel, Fairchild Semiconductor and Texas Instruments all refused. An executive at Texas Instruments took Amdahl aside and told him the idea would never work. Amdahl was unimpressed. In a 1996 interview, he said that part of his strategy was to leave more open areas on a single chip, decreasing problems with interconnection and making design automation much simpler.

"We were absolutely convinced that the failures that you would see were a function of the number of gates on the chip, not how big the chip was. We were making an extra-large chip so we would have the routing. But they couldn't get their mind off the way they normally do things, crowding everything together as tight as you can make it so you can get lots of chips on a wafer."[16]

Amdahl enlisted the help of Motorola Semiconductor Products and Advanced Memory System, Inc., to manufacture the circuits. Amdahl engineer John Zasio developed the chips and design automation.[17]

"When I looked at the technology compared to what everybody else was doing, it was a quantum leap forward," said Reed W. Larsen, hired in 1972 as design manager. By 1996, he was vice president of compatible systems development. "We really pioneered the idea of gate design." Amdahl's LSI chips were the predecessors of today's chips, which contain thousands of gates.[18]

David and Goliath

A small team of engineers worked 10-hour days, weekends included, to make Amdahl's vision a reality. Two people worked on instructions, four were in charge of execution, and four had responsibility for storage. The team included Lawrence J. Ellison, who, along with Robert Miner and Edward Oates, would found Oracle Systems Corporation in 1977. Ellison remains chairman and chief executive officer of the $7 billion software giant.

"People were excited about what they were doing," said Bill Flanagan, hired in 1973 as manager of production control. "You could just feel the excitement in the air."[19] The challenge was daunting. The system had to be better than IBM's, as well as completely compatible.

The real challenge, however, was hiring qualified people who could make the system work. Few people were willing to leave IBM to join a startup with a shaky future. A college recruitment program was established, but not many recent college graduates knew anything about the IBM architecture with which Amdahl's systems would be compatible.

But the informal atmosphere at Amdahl worked in the company's favor. Henry Cassel recalled that during his 12 years at Pacific Gas and Electric in San Francisco, he saw the CEO exactly twice. By contrast, when he moved to Amdahl in 1975, he met Gene Amdahl in the company cafeteria on his very first day. "There was this camaraderie," Cassel said. "The bond that made us a real team was a feeling that we were David fighting against Goliath."[20]

That David-and-Goliath feeling intensified in 1971 when IBM delivered its first System 370 Model 145 computer — the first computer system with a main memory containing monolithic integrated circuit technology. The system could write or read at a rate of 1.25 million characters per second on magnetic tape. At that pace, a 1,500-page dictionary would be synthesized in less than 13 seconds. The system was also capable of storing more than 262,000 characters of information on 131 circuit cards.[21] Perhaps most important of all, the S 370 became part of a family of computers that was compatible with the S 360. Consumers could upgrade their systems without scrapping all that expensive software.

The introduction of the S 370 had a major impact on the large-scale-computer industry.

presenting his case to anybody who would listen. He had a way of looking potential investors in the eye and telling his story with unswerving confidence. "I'm sure he worked out the problem of how to present this thing so the person he was talking to would sign the check," said Brewer.[23]

In March, representatives of Fujitsu in Japan expressed interest in Amdahl Corporation. Gene Amdahl had become friends with Dr. Toshio Ikeda, a respected engineer fondly known as Mr. Computer in Japan. Ikeda was more than six feet tall and had many Western mannerisms and ideas.

After a series of meetings and a trip to Japan by Gene Amdahl, Fujitsu agreed to

When IBM introduced the System 370 Model 145, several competitors dropped out of the mainframe business. Amdahl, however, was not intimidated.

Unable to compete with IBM, RCA and General Electric (GE) both closed their computer operations and left the large-scale market entirely. This turn of events must have been disquieting, but Gene Amdahl had no intention of giving up.[22]

Fujitsu, Limited

Throughout 1971, Amdahl contacted virtually every venture capital venue in the nation,

invest $5 million in Amdahl Corporation under a joint development agreement with licensing under Amdahl Corporation's patents. The agreement was concluded in the fall. Fujitsu's infusion of cash allowed Amdahl Corporation to complete the logical design of the machine.[24] Unfortunately, Ikeda would die suddenly in late 1973 before the computer reached the market. He was heavily involved in the project until his death.

Forming the circular part of the chip, heatsinks were used to keep the devices from melting.

Fujitsu, which would remain an important partner throughout the history of Amdahl, had been founded in 1935. "They are very traditional, and as a result, there are some very pronounced characteristics that come out of that," said Bert O'Neill, the longtime liaison between the two companies.

"On the positive side, they are very good partners as far as the question of trust is established. Their engineering and their ability given some base ideas to optimize them are very, very strong. On the other hand, in spite of what you may think, and there's some contradiction with the

other Japanese companies, they are just not a marketing company. In fact, it's against Japanese culture, in which the sales operation is considered to be akin to begging."[25]

Late in 1971, Fujitsu sent 10 designers and engineers to Amdahl Corporation's facilities in Sunnyvale to assist in developing the new computer system.[26] Amdahl's employees and the Fujitsu team worked well together. The Japanese engineers reported to Amdahl's managers and performed their tasks as regular Amdahl employees. The Americans enjoyed teaching their Japanese counterparts how to play touch football in the parking lot.[27]

Yoshiro Yoshioka, an engineer from Fujitsu who in 1996 would be general manager of Fujitsu's Open Systems Group, and who had served on Amdahl's board of directors in 1991 and 1992, said the two companies complemented each other. Amdahl provided the revolutionary design and technology, while Fujitsu was responsible for manufacturing and evaluation. "The combination of the two was a very good thing for the development," he said.[28]

Nixdorf

Throughout 1972, the technical staff continued working on what was to be known as the Amdahl 470/6 machine while Gene Amdahl continued his search for more financing. His efforts didn't pay off until September, when Nixdorf Computer of West Germany sent several technicians to evaluate Amdahl's plans and development progress. After two weeks of analysis, Heinz Nixdorf himself arrived at Amdahl's facilities. He liked what he saw and agreed to invest $6 million as a first step in negotiations for a business arrangement in Europe.

Nixdorf owned half of Telefunken Computers and wanted Amdahl Corporation to use components made by Telefunken in the 470/6. However, negotiations broke down when the Nixdorf people, unfamiliar with the high-end computer market, began to question Amdahl's market projections and technology.[29]

The situation had a silver lining. Amdahl Corporation still received the $6 million that had been invested before negotiations as a sign of Nixdorf's goodwill. Better yet, Fujitsu, Ltd., nervous about Nixdorf Computer's large investment and relationship with Amdahl Corporation, decided to invest another $6.2 million in the company. That investment, in addition to another $7.8 million from investors in the United States, brought $20 million into the coffers of Amdahl Corporation by October 1972. This third round of financing enabled Amdahl Corporation to build a prototype and prepare its manufacturing facilities for production.[30]

Operating expenses for the year had reached $5,466,000, representing a net loss of $5,555,000.[31] This was according to plan, and most employees remained deeply optimistic. "We were oblivious to the risk," Larsen said. "We just thought we were doing the funnest things that we could do."[32] Though some weeks were more of a struggle than others, the company never missed a pay period.

Employees were bolstered by Gene Amdahl's confidence. Early in 1973, he boasted to a reporter that "we are going to offer something so significantly better than IBM that it will be with great trepidation that a customer will decide not to go with us."[33] Meanwhile, Fujitsu committed an additional $35 million, bringing Amdahl Corporation's capitalization to $72.5 million.[34]

Gearing Up for Production

Anticipating the company's conversion from development to production, Amdahl Corporation leased 125,000 square feet of additional floor space in Sunnyvale and expected its number of employees to reach 500, mostly in manufacturing, by the end of the year.[35]

Sunnyvale was the ideal location for Amdahl Corporation. With the Vietnam War finally over, city leaders were seeking high-technology companies that manufactured products for the consumer market rather than for defense industries. Sixty electronics companies were already operating in Sunnyvale, and 43 additional industrial buildings were under construction.[36] The area was being

Building A, under construction in early 1974.

transformed into the high-tech, high-stress, traffic-clogged, big-money region known to the world as Silicon Valley.

In June 1973, Amdahl decided to seek the fourth and final round of financing through a public offering. It was a risky move because the stock market was far from bullish at the time. After Amdahl had secured one underwriter and prepared the necessary offering document for the Securities and Exchange Commission, the underwriter's securities holdings decreased to the point where he could no longer meet the obligation of adequate capitalization.

Amdahl decided to remain with private investors and spent July through September traveling throughout the United States, Canada and Europe in search of additional funding.[37] He carried with him the results of a study completed in July, which was based on interviews with 254 users of large-scale computers. The results were extremely promising. Seventy percent of respondents planned to install new computers between 1975 and 1977, and 32 percent would consider installing a system from a new company.

The study also showed what Amdahl already knew: It wouldn't be easy to convince potential customers to switch from a major brand name to an unknown company. IBM's domination of the market was near-total. Of the 254 computer users interviewed, only eight used non-IBM equipment. What would it take to make them switch? The study found that if the price of the alternative system was the same as IBM's, performance would have to be 20 percent better. If performance and reliability were the same, the price would have to be 20 percent less than a comparable IBM system. Potential customers said they were most interested in speed, reliability and compactness. Most important of all, according to 52 percent of those surveyed, was a system that didn't require software conversion. Nobody wanted to throw away expensive software and start from scratch.[38]

Another study of IBM 360 users completed in July 1973 found that 67 percent of respondents planned to change their central processing unit between December 1972 and December 1975. Amdahl was confident he could convince some of those people to buy something other than an IBM.[39]

An engineer tests the central processing unit of the 470V/6.

A Curve Ball

In mid-1973, IBM introduced a new system that utilized virtual memory, a feature that allowed more efficient and flexible use of main memory. Virtual memory allows an application to perceive the system as providing a large uniform primary memory, when in reality it might be smaller and more fragmented. Real memory, on the other hand, is the amount of memory actually existing in a system. For example, a computer could have 4 megabytes of RAM, but support a virtual memory of 20 megabytes.

Amdahl's system, although similar to the IBM 370, utilized real memory, not virtual memory.[40] When IBM announced its new product, Amdahl Corporation had already finished designing its own system and was in the process of debugging it.[41]

At first, Gene Amdahl didn't believe that the virtual memory system would have much impact on the market. He considered it inferior to the real memory system. But since customers liked virtual memory, Amdahl soon realized that the company had no choice but to stop working on the 470V/6 and begin developing a system that used the IBM model. It didn't make sense to devote any more energy to a system that would not be compatible with IBM's latest system.

The company had to switch gears — fast. Personnel were slashed from 800 to 400, with most of the cuts taking place in manufacturing. Engineering was reduced from 270 to 180 employees, and several levels of management were eliminated.[42]

Ed Cardinal, who joined Amdahl in 1972 after 14 years at IBM, was petrified. "I had six kids and had moved to California. I had quit this really solid company, and all of a sudden we didn't know if we were going to have jobs," he recalled. (Cardinal survived the cuts and in 1997 celebrated 25 years with Amdahl.)[43]

The engineers that were left had an enormous challenge on their hands. "We didn't know what the actual implementation of the virtual design was," said Bruce Beebe, hired from Mascor at the same time as Dave Brewer. Beebe, who retired in 1994 as senior vice president, was a development manager on the project. "We had to make our best guess as to what IBM was going to do architecturally, and then implement it. This is where Gene was very creative. He told us to be very flexible, so if we were wrong, we could change it quickly."[44]

However, the attitude on the design floor remained positive. Having already agreed to work for this long-shot company, the engineers and designers took this newest bump in the road in stride.

As they went back to the drawing board, Gene Amdahl continued his search for financing. Throughout November 1973, Amdahl met with many investment groups, again without success. In December, he held a luncheon in London. The guests arrived an hour late, looking miserable. The London Stock Exchange had dropped that morning to its lowest point since 1929. Money for Amdahl was out of the question.

Gene Amdahl returned to the United States, where he hoped an offering document that had

One innovation of the 470V/6 was multichip carriers with large-scale integration. The old system, an integrated circuit board, is shown in the background.

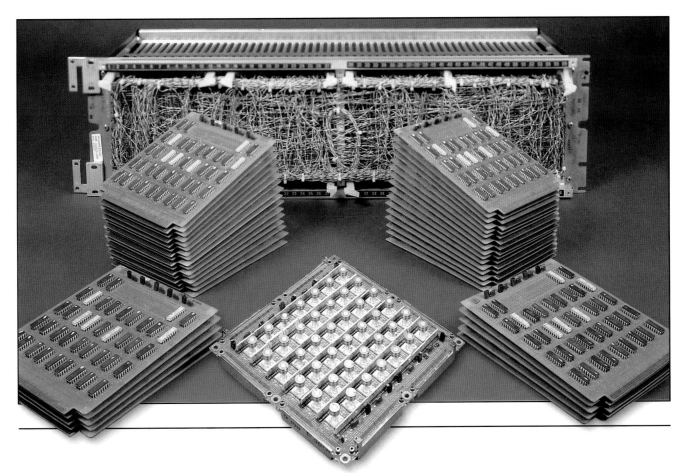

been submitted to the Securities and Exchange Commission at the end of October would be ready for announcement. Unfortunately, the inspector at the Securities and Exchange Commission left to join the President's Energy Council, forcing Amdahl to start the offering process all over again. Once again, he elected to remain with private funding.[45]

By the end of 1973, there was only enough money to last one month. Believing the end was near, five top executives left the company.

A Show of Loyalty

Early in 1974, the board of directors began expressing doubt about the management abilities of Gene Amdahl.[46] While it was true that Gene Amdahl was a better computer designer than CEO, he inspired a tremendous amount of loyalty. Most employees felt that they could not succeed without him. "We wouldn't be here without Gene," said Robert Maier, an Amdahl veteran since 1970. "He was everything."[47] If he left, the excitement of a start-up operation based on one man's vision would be gone.

On March 18, 274 employees from all levels of the company signed a statement expressing support for Gene Amdahl as president and his selection of Bob Armstrong as the chief operating officer.

"We, the undersigned, feel a commitment to the long-term growth of the Amdahl Corporation. To this end, we support Dr. Gene M. Amdahl as President and Chairman of the Board, and his selection of Mr. R.W. Armstrong as Chief Operating Officer. We are confident that Dr. Amdahl will manage the Company in a way which will make it a success in the eyes of the stockholders and provide us with an acceptable working environment. We feel that it is essential that Dr. Amdahl and Mr. Armstrong participate jointly in any negotiations which deal with the future of Amdahl Corporation.

Since we share with them a common goal for the future of the Amdahl Corporation, the undersigned will resign from the Company if either Dr. Amdahl or Mr. Armstrong should resign during the present negotiations because he feels the goal cannot be achieved."[48]

Anderson signed his name first. "He was a legend," Anderson said, explaining his support for Gene Amdahl. "I mean, he designed the 360 at IBM. He was the founder of the company."[49] Gene Amdahl brought the document with him to Japan, where he was meeting with top executives at Fujitsu. In the midst of what was equivalent to a board meeting, Amdahl dropped the statement on the table.[50] Although Amdahl would no longer be CEO, he would remain president of the company. Bob Armstrong, tragically, would die a few months later in a scuba diving accident.[51]

Eugene R. White

Amdahl was a brilliant man, but it was clear that the company, without a chief operating officer, needed somebody to take control of day-to-day

Eugene R. White was hired in 1974 as president of the company. He would become deputy chairman in 1977 and then be promoted to chairman and chief executive officer in 1979, positions he held until 1987 and 1983, respectively. He was serving as vice chairman at the time of his retirement in 1993.

Gene Amdahl in front of Building A in 1974. "We are going to offer something so much better than IBM that it will be with great trepidation that a customer will decide not to go with us," he said.

operations. To fill this need, Eugene R. White was named president of the company in August 1974.[52] White, with a strong background in both technology and management, would eventually become chairman and CEO of the company. He retired as vice chairman in 1993.

Born and raised in Bangor, Maine, White earned a physics degree from the University of Maine. After serving as a captain in the U.S. Army, he joined GE in 1959 as a design engineer on nuclear reactors. Recognized as an employee with high management potential, he soon became task supervisor at GE's Aircraft Nuclear Department. In 1966, while only 34 years old, he was named engineering manager for GE's Computer Systems Equipment groups, in charge of 1,300 engineers and programmers.

When General Electric decided to sell its computer business, White served on the corporate task force that negotiated the 1970 sale to Honeywell. It was one of the largest mergers in history, cre-

ating what was then the world's second-largest computer company. As part of the negotiations, Honeywell requested that White join the company. He agreed to a year-long commitment, becoming vice president of engineering and manufacturing integration at the newly formed Honeywell Information Systems.

When the year was up, White decided to move to the West Coast, where he joined Fairchild Camera & Instrument Company, as vice president of the Commercial Equipment Group. The company was going through a difficult financial period, and White was instrumental in turning it around. In 1974, he left the company, hoping to start his own venture-capital business.

Meanwhile, E.F. Heizer, who knew White only through reputation, asked White if he would spend some time at Amdahl Corporation and tell him if the company was worth further investment. In February 1974, White became a consultant for Amdahl.

"I was very intrigued. I was in the business of competing against IBM at GE and Honeywell, so I knew how difficult it was. I had never been exposed to a compatibility strategy before.

"I had been exposed to a lot of technology and of course my degree was in physics. I thought the technology was quite intriguing and potentially viable, so I reported to Heizer that I thought with the right management and leadership Amdahl had something that could potentially be a winner, although it was way behind schedule.

"I told him it would probably take another 18 months and another million dollars a month. If he was going to put any more money in, he should be prepared to put in his share of the $18 million."[53]

White also met with Fujitsu executives, convincing them to contribute more to Amdahl. The

A large logic simulator, created in-house at Amdahl, helped engineers iron out bugs in the system.

executives wanted White to take over the company, but White declined, saying he still wanted to start a venture capital concern.

"However, I agreed to get it organized, get it off the ground and help get things set up so they could raise more money. Then they could hire a president.

"I did that, and they kept looking for somebody, and nobody seemed right. Eventually they kept pressuring me and finally I decided to put aside my personal plans for three years."[54]

White asked Heizer and Fujitsu to contribute the full $18 million needed to get the first computer to market. By the end of the year, the two companies contributed a total of $17.3 million.

At the time, the company was struggling each week to meet payroll. White immediately began

making the tough but necessary decisions that would put the company on the right track. One of the first things he did was clamp down on expenses, which had climbed to $14.6 million in 1973.[55] "When Gene [White] arrived, I remember saying that it became difficult to get a pencil if you didn't need it," said David L. Anderson, who joined the company in 1971 and was vice president and chief technology officer at the time of his retirement in 1999. "And people loved it. All of a sudden, we began running much more efficiently. We began planning out schedules."[56]

Most of 1974 would be spent developing and debugging the virtual memory version of the machine now known as the 470V/6.[57] Much of the testing for the new virtual machine was done on an enormous logic simulator built by Amdahl engineers.

In September, the company issued a news release announcing the development of a fourth-generation computer system available for business and scientific applications. It would be identical to IBM's virtual system but with a greater operating speed. By November of 1974, development of the 470V/6 was complete.[58]

But Gene Amdahl did not want to release the system until it was absolutely perfect. He knew that customers were skittish about switching suppliers, and the slightest operating difficulty would send them scurrying back to IBM.

Before it went on the market, the 470V/6 was put through intensive tests by customers. The first tests, by a German computer expert, were so successful that they led to two installations in West Germany. "This care in making certain that the first machines to be installed in the market would perform reliably may well be one of the most important decisions that governed the future acceptance of Amdahl products," Gene Amdahl later commented.[59]

By the end of the year, the company had leased four buildings with 200,000 square feet of floor space on 21 acres. Twenty-six patent applications had been filed in the data processing field, with 10 United States patents issued. Amdahl Corporation employed 290 people, of which 180 were professionals and 43 were managers with an aggregate of 390 years' experience.[60]

The close of 1974 brought with it the close of the first chapter in Amdahl Corporation's history. It had been a challenging period, fraught with financial pressures, industry surprises and management challenges. With the approach of 1975, the people of Amdahl Corporation were ready to see their hard work pay off. The company was finally ready to put its first computer on the market.

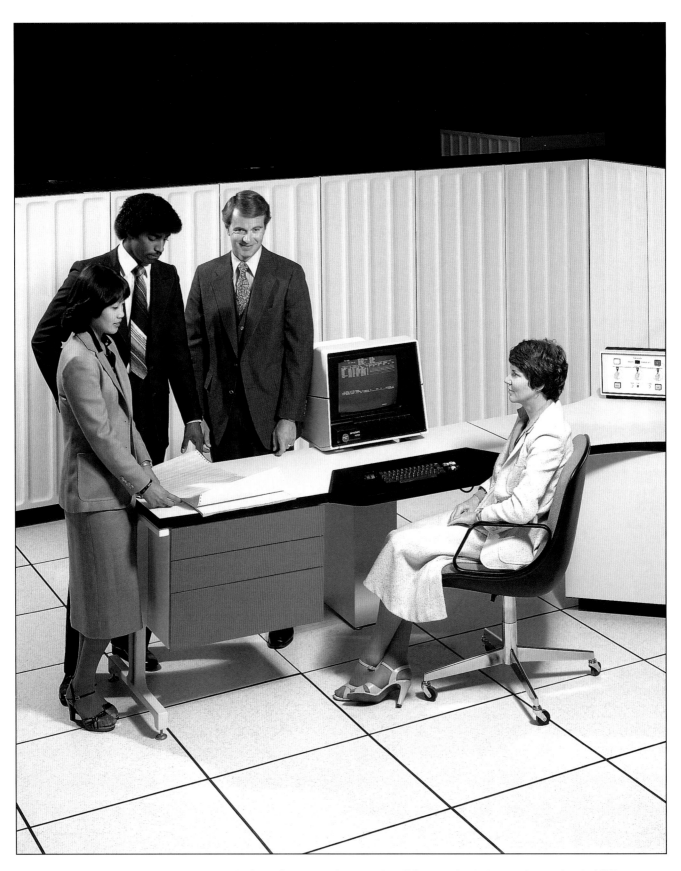

After four years of development, the 470V/6 was finally ready for the market. This promotional photograph was taken in 1975.

CHAPTER THREE

THE LAUNCH
1975

"We had to have an impeccable reputation for service, support, directness and honesty in dealing with our customers."

— James Dutton, vice president of eastern operations[1]

ENGINEERS AT AMDAHL Corporation spent the first few months of 1975 feverishly testing and evaluating the performance of the 470V/6. Any mistake would be fatal to the company's reputation, so all performance failures and equipment problems had to be solved before the first system was shipped.

The manufacturing department was extremely busy. The 470V/6 required more than 100 custom-made devices, including specially designed tools for removing circuit boards from the computer chassis. Assemblers needed three to four months of training before they could even begin to work on the assembly line.[2]

Curiosity was high about the potential success of the 470V/6 and, by extension, Amdahl Corporation. One headline in *Computer Decisions* magazine asked the question that was on many minds: "Has Amdahl Got A Billion Dollar Baby?"[3] Analysts speculated that IBM would have to develop a new line to be competitive or, at the very least, take a serious look at its price structure.

Amdahl Corporation's initial marketing strategy was to approach large institutions that operated multiple computer systems, on the theory that these companies could absorb the risk of trying something new. But this plan had a flaw, said Ray Williams, chief financial officer during the company's first two years. Large companies generally had elaborate purchasing policies that were risk-aversive. Some executives even worried that if they turned to lower-priced machines, the public would think the company was in trouble.

"You have to remember, the bigger the customer, the less likely it would be that he would be dealing with his own money.... We had much better luck when the boss who was going to buy the machine also owned the company or thought of it as his own. Then, the million bucks he saved was his."[4]

One sales technique was to give a presentation in which the characteristics of the IBM 370/168 and the Amdahl 470V/6 were listed on a chalkboard. After the lists were complete, the salesperson would write "Amdahl" over one column and "IBM" over the other. "The superior product was obvious," said James Dutton, vice president of Eastern operations. Amdahl's 470V/6 was about

---

The multichip carrier board, which simplified the connections among devices, was one of the unique features of the 470V/6.

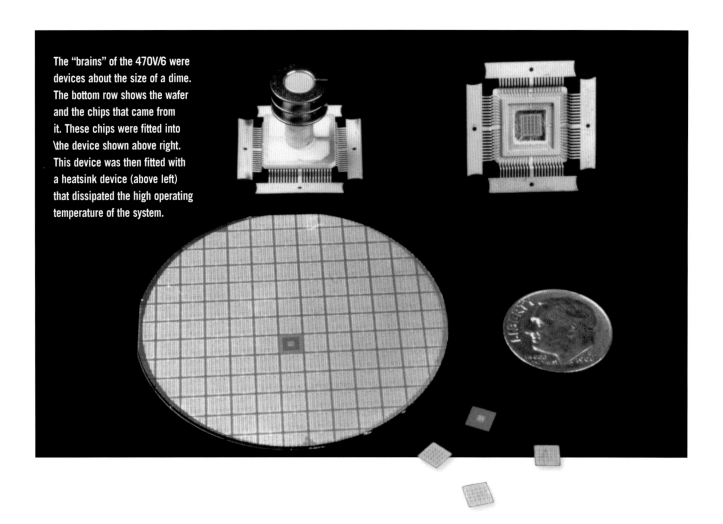

The "brains" of the 470V/6 were devices about the size of a dime. The bottom row shows the wafer and the chips that came from it. These chips were fitted into \the device shown above right. This device was then fitted with a heatsink device (above left) that dissipated the high operating temperature of the system.

May 1975 — Amdahl sells its first 470V/6 to the NASA Goddard Institute for Space Studies.

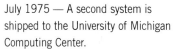

July 1975 — A second system is shipped to the University of Michigan Computing Center.

October 1975 — Texas A&M takes delivery on a 470V/6.

half the size of the IBM 168. It was between 1.4 and 1.8 times more powerful and cost 8 percent to 12 percent less. The 470V/6's air-cooling system, unlike the water-cooling system used in IBM computers, could save a customer as much as $250,000 in plumbing and related installation costs.[5]

Despite the obvious advantages of the Amdahl system, potential customers were nervous about alienating IBM by engaging an untested competitor. They wondered if Amdahl Corporation would be around long enough to support the product. "It was a situation where it didn't matter if you had the best mouse trap in the world because you were selling against the IBM corporation," recalled Ken Simonds, who left IBM in 1975 to become Amdahl's vice president of Western operations.[6]

President Gene White took a personal role in countering these concerns. "I had to look every customer right in the eye and say, 'I give you a personal commitment. We'll be there when you need us,'" he said.[7]

White was a strong believer in after-sale support, noting that "customers are counting on the fact that your organization will be able to service and support their installation."[8]

Gene Amdahl stands with the 470V/6. His vision had finally become a reality.

November 1975 — Computer Usage Company in California becomes an Amdahl customer.

December 1975 — Massachusetts Mutual Life Insurance Company receives a system.

December 1975 — A 470V/6 is purchased by the University of Alberta in Canada.

1975 — The Amdahl Diagnostic Assistance Center (AMDAC) is established.

To back up his words, he promised that spare parts would be sent with each new system to ensure quick repairs. In addition, Fujitsu Ltd. guaranteed all maintenance agreements. Those agreements became known as the Fujitsu Amendment. "That really helped, because while people had a lot of concern as to how long Amdahl might be around, there was no doubt that Fujitsu would be around," said Charlie Pratt, who joined Amdahl in 1975 and was in charge of sales in the western United States.[9]

By mid-May, Amdahl had its first sale.

Amdahl's First Customer

The NASA Goddard Institute for Space Studies in New York needed additional computer speed to process anticipated data from its next Nimbus satellite.[10] The machine would convert meteorological information to digital data, then analyze it. Amdahl Corporation, of course, wanted to supply the computer. But during negotiations, the company had at least two strikes against it. First, the institute, like other potential customers, already had an IBM system in operation. Second, Amdahl Corporation did not have time to follow the required standard government bidding procedures.[11] An Amdahl software engineer remembered, "We were a little naive about how we did business back then. This was a government installation, which meant we should have a bid in. Instead, we just showed up with our machine in a truck."[12]

NASA selected the 470V/6 because it was 2.5 times faster than the IBM 370/165 already being used at Goddard. To get the same speed from IBM, NASA would have had to purchase the IBM 370/195, which was double the price of the 470V/6 and took up much more floor space.[13]

After five years of being told that it couldn't be done, Amdahl Corporation had sold its first system.

Amdahl's first installation was at the NASA Goddard Institute for Space Studies in New York. NASA chose the machine because it was faster than a comparable IBM system, and employees at Goddard never regretted the decision.

That sale changed the large-scale computing industry forever. For the first time, customers had a choice. Competition within the industry could only lead to improved products, services and prices.

The day the system left Sunnyvale, the company threw a big party. Their spirits buoyed by champagne, employees watched as the 470V/6 was carefully loaded into the truck. Having come this far, the company took no chances when it came to shipping. An employee accompanied the truck to ensure the system would arrive undamaged in New York. A manufacturing employee was also sent in case configuration changes were needed during installation.[14]

The company even arranged the boxes in the truck so that they could be unloaded in the proper installation order at the customer's facilities.[15]

Production Control Manager Bill Flanagan was amazed by the number of details that needed attention. Things like serial number labels and patent labels, which had fallen to the bottom of the priority list while the 470V/6 was being developed, suddenly became very important.[16]

The Goddard Institute was housed in an old brownstone building near Columbia University. Amdahl's field engineers installed the first 470V/6 and had it running the customer's programs within five days — an impressive feat considering that IBM usually required two or three weeks.[17] On June 9, 1975, at 12:30 in the afternoon, the machine was turned on. After five years as a paper competitor to IBM, Amdahl had arrived.

Spreading the Word

With its first successful installation, Amdahl Corporation hoped that word of the landmark event would spread throughout the industry.[18] Luckily, Amdahl's first customers became the company's biggest supporters, said Dutton. "Once they had jumped into the pool, they wanted more people in the pool."[19] Another advantage for Amdahl was that it offered discounts, said Joe Francesconi, who was in charge of Chicago sales at the time. "Actually, in the early days, discounting was really a cosmetic thing. It didn't throw off the numbers at all. It was more that Amdahl could do it. IBM wouldn't even talk about discounts."[20]

Gene White, right, discusses the newly installed 470V/6 with the director of the University of Michigan Computing Center. The center had purchased a 470V/6 in July 1975.

In July, Amdahl Corporation shipped its second machine to the University of Michigan Computing Center. Amdahl's field staff had the 470V/6 up and running in less than a day and a half.[21]

During this particular installation, the air conditioner in the Computing Center malfunctioned. In an overheated room, the 470V/6, like all computers, would not function properly. One of the Amdahl field engineers removed the vacuum hose from his car and installed it in the air conditioner, thus keeping the room cool for several days.[22] This ingenious solution proved to the customer that Amdahl personnel "had a missionary fervor about what [they] were doing."[23]

When the system arrived, Dr. Robert Bartels, director of the University of Michigan Computing Center, could barely contain his excitement. "Although he was well into his 60s, he ran around like crazy, helped to unload the truck, pushed the machines around, operated the elevator — things

With a successful product on the market, Amdahl continued to expand its facilities throughout the second half of the seventies.

CHAPTER FOUR

FIGHTING FEAR, UNCERTAINTY AND DOUBT

1976–1977

"The early days of selling felt like a war zone. Our salesmen would go out and march up that hill — often returning with empty briefcases — and we all felt it. It was like a family we shared. When contracts began to be signed, we all savored the success, everyone from engineering to the receptionists and the people in manufacturing."

— Amdahl Update, 1990[1]

SALESMEN HAD NO PROBLEM securing appointments with potential customers of the 470V/6. Gene Amdahl was well known in the industry, and there was widespread curiosity about the company that was crazy enough to take on IBM.[2]

As sales activity intensified, nobody was surprised that IBM began to fight back. Gene Amdahl dubbed IBM's strategy "FUD," an acronym for the Fear, Uncertainty and Doubt that IBM tried to sow in potential Amdahl customers, noted Peter Williams, who became general manager of Amdahl's European operations in 1977, after 17 years with IBM in the United Kingdom. Williams, who retired in 1991, said Amdahl first used the term during a London presentation. Today, FUD is an accepted acronym that is even used as a verb, as in, "to FUD someone."[3]

When IBM officials learned they were in danger of losing an account to Amdahl, they would dispatch high-ranking representatives to the location to persuade the customer to stay with IBM. "In the beginning, their strategy was to make it very difficult [for customers to leave IBM]," said Bill O'Connell, who joined Amdahl in 1977 and retired as senior vice president in 1994.[4]

Perhaps the biggest concern of potential Amdahl customers was that IBM would not maintain its equipment if it was attached to Amdahl

systems. This IBM policy backfired by allowing Amdahl to take the high road and offer superior service and support. William Ferone, who joined Amdahl in 1978 and rose to become vice president and general manager of customer services, said the company always believed that "a customer's problem was an Amdahl problem."

"We found out very early that the best possible stance for us to take is that all problems were our problems. From the very first day we started shipping, we took that position in the marketplace and with our customers so they didn't have to be concerned about pointing fingers. We would take care of it. When we recruit people, there's never any discussion about who owns the problem. We just drill this into them from the day we start recruiting them. We tell them, 'You're with our customers. We don't want any argument. We don't want any finger pointing. You have one kind of commitment. You have one kind of attitude, and that is that the customer's problem is your problem.' And it's really instilled."[5]

Amdahl's 470V/6 was completely compatible with IBM's 370/158, shown above.

That attitude helped sell a lot of machines, said John Matthews, a support technician who had recently moved from IBM and was well aware of the differences between the two companies.

"When we sold a machine, the customer that made the decision to buy it was putting his job on the line. If it didn't work, that guy could lose his job. If it did work, he saved a few million dollars. He bought something that was faster. He might be a little bit of a hero, but being a hero on one side and getting fired on the other was not a good balance. So we did everything we could to try to make the customer successful."[6]

As Amdahl sales people became accustomed to the FUD strategy, they were able to minimize its impact by telling customers what to expect

Amdahl customers soon learned that a casually placed Amdahl coffee mug could prompt IBM to offer massive savings on its machines.

from IBM. When Fear, Uncertainty and Doubt didn't work, IBM slashed its prices.[7] A popular myth developed about the Million Dollar Coffee Mug. When Amdahl executives visited potential customers, they often gave away mugs adorned with the Amdahl corporate logo. A few executives realized that if they oh-so-casually placed these mugs on their desks during negotiations, IBM would knock $1 million off the price of a mainframe.[8]

Amdahl's lawyers also fought IBM's stronghold on state government contracts, remembered Fred Gonzalez, who joined Amdahl in 1978 and rose to the rank of associate general counsel of operations.

"Beginning around the end of 1978, we engaged in a rather aggressive attempt to break open the state government marketplace with a series of state government protest activities. At one time, I think we had six or seven of these going on simultaneously. What would happen is that the government would come out with a request for proposal with certain criteria for eval-

August 1976 — Amdahl becomes a public company.

December 1976 — Construction begins on a fifth Amdahl building in Sunnyvale.

December 1976 — Amdahl International is formed as a joint venture with Fujitsu, Ltd.

uation of bids. When they realized that our bid was lower, they would try to slant the evaluation in favor of IBM." [9]

In this intensely competitive atmosphere, Amdahl salespeople were aware that their efforts had historical significance. "We had an opportunity to change an industry," said Ollie J. Nutt, a former IBM marketing manager who became regional manager for sales in the Houston region in 1976. [10]

Wayne McIntyre, a Chicago account executive and former IBM salesman, said that succeeding became "a mission because IBM was so arrogant."

"I had an IBM vice president tell me, in as condescending a tone as you can imagine, that the streets were littered with the bodies of people who thought they could compete with IBM. Most of us had one of those guys lurking over us, and we wanted to make them eat those words." [11]

McIntyre got his chance a few years later. After winning an account, he ran into the very same vice president in the hall of the customer's headquarters. If he had had a knife and fork with him, he would have handed them over.

Gathering Momentum

Amdahl shipped seven machines during the first two quarters of 1976 and 27 by the end of the year. [12] Ten were installed in industrial and commercial environments, and 17 were used to support scientific and government facilities.

At one installation, the 470V/6 system supervised 120 die-casting machines, monitoring as many as five quality and quantity functions twice per second for each machine. The system handled more than 3 million transactions per hour, which was less than one percent of its capabilities. [13]

Field technicians held informal competitions to see who could install systems the fastest. Working in shifts, they could install the machines in less than 24 hours, with the record standing at eight hours. [14] The quick installations got relationships with customers off to a good start.

Some installations were more difficult than others. In one instance, field technicians arrived in Connecticut only to find an elevator too narrow to accommodate the 470V/6. In order to get the system to its destination, a hole had to be knocked out of the second-floor exterior wall, and ramps had to be constructed from the ground to the

1976 — Amdahl sells 27 systems during the year.

August 1977 — Jack Lewis is hired as president of Amdahl.

1977 — Amdahl expands the 470 family with three products.

May 1978 — Amdahl begins building a manufacturing facility in a suburb of Dublin, Ireland.

hole.[15] Faced with the same problem at a facility in West Germany later that year, engineers used a crane to hoist the 470V/6 to its destination.[16] Such extraordinary efforts helped win the confidence of new customers.[17]

Less than 18 months after the 470V/6 was introduced, Amdahl had recouped all of the capital that had been invested in five years of research and development. Customers were realizing that competition improved both prices and service, said account executive Wayne McIntyre. In the past, backlogs had forced some IBM customers to wait as long as two years for a system. But if IBM representatives knew that Amdahl was competing for a customer, delivery delays would magically disappear.

One customer kept a chart of machine reliability, with IBM represented in blue and Amdahl represented in red. Whichever color was on top when it was time to buy a new system would get the order, said McIntyre. "Of course, what he was doing was playing off the two service and support organizations. Each wanted to make sure that its line was above the other guy's." As it turned out, the customer never purchased the next machine.[18]

Going Public

In August 1976, Amdahl Corporation became a public company through an initial public offering. The initial offering was supposed to be $32.50 per share, but the Securities and Exchange Commission agent handling the offering went on vacation. His substitute, who was unfamiliar with the project, delayed the offer a week. Because of market changes, the price dropped to $27.50. "That week cost us $5 million," said Ed Thompson, hired in 1976 as CEO of Amdahl Capital Corporation.[19] The offering generated $25 million, increasing the net worth of the company to $80 million.[20]

"It was a major success story for the company, "said Gene Plonka, a key finance figure in the company. "The confidence level that existed in the marketplace for Amdahl was very important."[21]

Before the offering, Gene Amdahl had argued that he should be reinstated as CEO of the company, a position that had been vacant since 1974. He pointed out that his name and reputation would boost credibility with analysts, and he threatened to leave the company if he did not get the job. As a result, Amdahl and Gene White agreed to share the CEO position, as White later explained:

"I thought his name was valuable and a big benefit from the standpoint of marketing. The directors were trying to decide if they would push him out or keep him. I convinced both Gene and the board that he should stay. I cut a deal with him that I wouldn't advertise myself as the CEO and he could be chairman."[22]

IBM's vaunted 370/158 (above) and 370/155 (left) found themselves in unexpected competition with Amdahl's 470V/6, which was both cheaper and faster.

Amdahl International

The money raised from the public offering allowed the company to expand its organization. To supplement its six sales offices, the company established spare part depots in cities that had several Amdahl systems.[23] Toward the end of 1976, construction began on a fifth Sunnyvale building that would house manufacturing and a new research and development lab.[24]

Amdahl International, based in Europe, was formed as a joint venture with Fujitsu to oversee international operations. Two subsidiaries were formed — Amdahl, Limited, of Canada was headquartered in Toronto with a regional office in Montreal, and Amdahl Deutschland GmbH was based in West Germany.

One of the subsidiary's early sales was to Swiss Railways, said Steve Coggins, a salesman who became marketing director for Europe in 1983. "They bought a machine, and they housed it in this computer room located over a railroad track. We had an intermittent problem there that we couldn't fix for months. In the end, we traced it to one particular locomotive that was giving off some sort of energy whenever it passed underneath this computer room. It was very random and very rare, but every time it passed, the whole computer collapsed." After Amdahl's support group tracked down the source, Swiss Railways remedied the problem by fixing the electrical connections within the train — there was no problem with the Amdahl computer.[25]

Even in Europe, customers insisted on meeting with senior Amdahl management. To clinch a sale in Norway, Gene Amdahl sang the only Norwegian song he knew, the Norwegian National Anthem. "Though I have the voice of a frog, I made more money than Frank Sinatra ever did for performing just one song," he told *Fortune* magazine.[26] The company established Amdahl Norge A/S Norway to accommodate customers in the homeland of Amdahl's grandparents.[27]

The rivalry with IBM stretched to the far corners of the globe. At one event, officials of Amdahl Europe attended a sales meeting in

Left: Amdahl executives playfully examine the 470V/7 after it is installed at Western Electric.

Below: The design team of the 470V/7. The system was introduced in March 1977.

Iceland, recalled Alan Bell, who was in charge of the European service organization at the time and later became general manager of European operations and then president of the Amdahl Global Solutions Group.

"One night they were coming home from a nightclub and they happened to pass the IBM headquarters. They could see the IBM flag two floors up, on a flat roof. So they climbed the flagpole, took the IBM flag and replaced it with an Amdahl tie on the top of the flagpole. They brought that flag back, and it used to hang in the Norwegian office."[28]

Recruiting talented employees was one of the company's top priorities. "A company is only as good as its people," noted White. Employees were attracted by the chance to beat IBM at its own game, without the bureaucracy of the larger organization.[29]

However, it was more difficult to recruit employees in Europe than in the United States. Most of the serious prospects worked at IBM, which was still considered the only game in town. Given a choice between a secure job and two guys conducting interviews in a hotel room, prospects usually chose the security of IBM.

At that point in time, Amdahl Corporation was so informal that it lacked even a controller or chief executive officer. In fact, the bylaws did not even refer to a CEO, since Amdahl and White shared the various responsibilities of the position.[30]

But the informality was attractive to some European recruits. Peter Williams recalled that while IBM employees dressed in conservative suits and ties, Amdahl's staff was more casual. The installation teams would even wear T-shirts and jeans. A favorite T-shirt, which was given to customers as well as employees, featured a tiny man with a pick axe, struggling to scale an enormous mountain. The figure, dressed in red, represented Amdahl, rising in the computer industry despite tremendous odds.[31]

The company turned a profit for the first time in 1976, with income of $22.7 million on sales of

A 470V/7, before being sent to Manufacturers' Life in Canada.

$92.8 million.[32] In one year, the size of the staff more than doubled, increasing from 373 to 770.[33]

Expanding the 470 Family

In March 1977, IBM responded to Amdahl Corporation's success by announcing the introduction of the IBM 3033 processor, which would be nearly twice as fast as its 370/168 and 30 percent cheaper. As frosting on the cake, IBM also enacted a 30 percent price reduction for its large mainframe systems, such as the model 370/168 — the chief competitor to the 470V/6. IBM made this announcement on a Friday afternoon.

Bert O'Neill, who worked for the marketing division of IBM at the time and moved to Amdahl in 1980, remembered that "the group I was in managed to hoodwink IBM's management" by providing deceptively low performance statistics. Since IBM had a strict price/performance structure, management set the price based on the false report. "Then we came back afterwards and said, 'We ran these tests, and it happens to be running faster.'"[34]

By Monday morning, Amdahl Corporation was ready to respond with what was later described as "the fastest major business decision of 1977."[35] On March 28, the company announced the introductions of the 470V/7 and the 470V/5. The 470V/7 would be 1.4 times as powerful as the IBM 3033.[36] The 470V/5 would be a trimmed-down version of the V/7, about the same speed as the IBM 370/168-3, and three times as fast as the IBM 370/158-3.[37] Both systems would be available in the second half of 1978.

Amdahl also announced a price reduction in the 470V/6 product line that maintained the system's price/performance ratio over the IBM 370/168.[38]

The company was steadily gaining prestige. In May 1977, Gene Amdahl was honored with the Michelson/Morley Award for his outstanding accomplishments as an engineer. The award was presented by the Case Institute of Technology during its annual meeting in Cleveland, Ohio. The Case Institute, supported by 60 corporations, recognized and encouraged the technological achievements of scientists and engineers.[39]

The following month, Amdahl Corporation began construction on a semiconductor processing lab in Building M3 of its growing Sunnyvale complex. The lab would be used to study new technologies and develop high-speed integrated circuits.[40]

Jack Lewis

Amdahl Corporation had grown so quickly that it needed to organize its corporate structure. In August 1977, John "Jack" Lewis was hired as president. Lewis had earned a bachelor's degree in accounting from California State University in Fresno. After a three-year tour of duty as an officer in the U.S. Navy, he began his corporate career in 1960 as a salesman for IBM's Service Bureau Corporation. Lewis quickly became the organization's top salesman and was promoted several times. In 1970, he joined Xerox Corporation, becoming vice president of marketing for Xerox Data Systems in 1973 and president of that organization one year later. By 1976, he had been named

Jack Lewis (standing), hired in August 1977 as president of Amdahl, and Gene White, who became deputy chairman of the company.

president of Xerox Business Systems, in charge of virtually everything except copiers.

Xerox headquarters were in Southern California, and Gene White called Lewis several times asking if he would join Amdahl Corporation as president. White, who still had dreams of starting his own venture capital firm, strongly hinted that Lewis could eventually run the company. Lewis turned down the offer two or three times but finally agreed to meet with White and review the company's potential.

"I was a very senior executive at Xerox, and if I stayed with it I would have a lot of moving to do. My wife and I liked it in California, our children were in junior high and grade school, and we didn't want to move them around a lot. After a long and agonizing thought process, I decided to take a flier on this thing.

"It was an opportunity to stay in California and an opportunity to develop a company on my own."[41]

Lewis' first priority was to bring structure to the expanding organization. "It was a rapidly growing company that had no processes or procedures," he recalled.

"Everyone did everything. My job was to try to get processes and systems in place that would allow us to continue to grow without introducing a whole set of bureaucracies that would stifle the growth. That was the management challenge. The technical challenge was making sure the development of the technology in the company stayed ahead of the competition."[42]

Lewis also had strong ideas about the kind of culture he wanted to foster at Amdahl. While creating formal procedures, Lewis was careful to limit bureaucracies that would impede the flow of ideas.

"We had to make sure we created a fun environment where we could retain highly competent technical people who would be challenged. We wanted to give people a lot more authority than they might have in other kinds of companies."[43]

Determined not to become isolated from employees, Lewis made a habit of eating lunch in the employee cafeteria and held frequent informal meetings with 15 to 20 randomly selected employees. A month after he joined Amdahl, Lewis was elected to the board of directors.

A Presence in Ireland

Not long after Lewis arrived, the company announced plans to build a manufacturing facility in Dublin, Ireland. "We started right out telling ourselves we would be a multinational corporation," Lewis said.[44] The Irish government promised to provide training funds, tax incentives and personnel assistance for what would become the first nonunion factory in Ireland.[45]

Another advantage to the facility in Ireland was that it would appease some European customers who were reluctant to buy Japanese products. Executives at Philips' Gloeilampenfabrieken, for example, refused to buy a 470V/6 because it contained components manufactured by Fujitsu, Limited. But they would consider purchasing a system produced in Ireland.[46]

An interim facility opened on May 24, 1978, in Glasnevin, a suburb of Dublin. The permanent facility in Swords, Ireland, opened in 1980. The plant manufactured the complete line of 470 computers, systems that required more than 25,000 parts.[47]

As part of its growing interest in Europe, Amdahl Corporation established Amdahl A.G. in Zurich, Switzerland, and Amdahl France S.A.R.L. in Paris. It also opened offices in Middlesex, England, under the supervision of Amdahl, Limited.[48]

These subsidiaries improved installation efficiency in Europe, where metric measurements and a different electrical system presented challenges to engineers accustomed to domestic installations. In addition, environmental standards tended to be tougher, shipments had to be made by air as well as land, and customer contracts were subject to local laws that varied from city to province.[49]

Financial returns for 1977 showed that revenue had increased 103 percent, to nearly $189 million, while income had increased 126 percent, to $26.7 million. Amdahl was gaining credibility. It had sold systems to each of the Big Three automakers and was enjoying a strong repeat business. One

Above and right: Trainees prepare to work at Amdahl's new manufacturing facility in Dublin, Ireland.

out of every four systems that left Amdahl facilities went to an established customer.[50]

But as Jack Lewis pointed out, the company should have done even better. "When you've got a product that's superior in every way, and you still can't get more than 15 percent of the marketplace at most, that tells you something about the power of your competition."[51]

Still, Amdahl had proved that it could succeed in a market dominated by a global giant. Imitation, the highest form of flattery, was inevitable. By the end of the year, competitors had entered the IBM-compatible market that Amdahl had invented, although none were as successful.[52]

In the late seventies, Amdahl evolved from a start-up company to a growing corporation. The company's new headquarters, symbolizing this change, was completed in 1978.

CHAPTER FIVE

GROWTH & TRANSITION
1978–1980

"The challenges we are facing in 1978 are related to the management tasks of controlled growth."

— Jack Lewis, 1978[1]

AMDAHL CORPORATION HEADED into 1978 from a position of strength, boasting an established reputation and a positive balance sheet. True to predictions, the worldwide market for mainframe computers was pushing sales of the 470V/6 ever upward. Amdahl established itself as a technological innovator and plowed money into new product development and acquisition. Instead of worrying about going out of business, corporate officers now faced a new challenge: how to take Amdahl from a research-driven manufacturing firm to a computer company selling a product. As Jack Lewis recalled, the transition from engineering innovator into marketing company wasn't always easy — especially in an industry dominated by "one of the fine corporations of the world."[2]

But it was an exciting, and sometimes slightly unhinged, period. The company had aimed at the most sophisticated computer market in the world and was succeeding — yet invoices were still tapped out on manual typewriters.[3] To cover the rapid growth, Amdahl was hiring people as fast as possible and building new facilities at a breakneck pace. Ernest B. Thompson, hired as controller in late 1978, recalled that the company was rapidly implementing "policies, procedures, systems and financial infrastructure that ... anticipate being a much bigger company."[4] Revenues in 1978 soared to more than $320 million, up from $189 million the year before, and employment mushroomed to nearly 3,000.[5]

With demand strong, Amdahl wasted no time in expanding its physical facilities. A two-story, 54,000-square-foot corporate headquarters was built, and 41,000 square feet of manufacturing space were added. A new facility, called Building M4, was erected for testing and assembly. Another building, O-5, under construction a short distance from the main Amdahl Corporation campus, would be used for storage, receiving and testing when it opened in January 1979. Other off-site construction included the 129,000-square-foot Building O-7[6] and the 51,000-square-foot Building O-6.[7] Beginning in early 1977, construction teams worked 16- and 18-hour days to meet the company's demand for more space.[8]

The company also opened new field sales offices in St. Louis, Missouri,[9] and Denver, Colorado,[10] and a center for product support and services was established in Columbia, Maryland, in 1980.[11]

As the company gained recognition, it found its 470 chip on the April 12, 1980, cover of *World Business Weekly*.

The new buildings quickly filled with new employees. At one point, the company hired an average of 40 employees per week.[12] "In those days, we would hire as many people in a year as we started out the year with," recalled Tony Pozos, who joined Amdahl in 1976 as vice president of industrial relations.[13] The production control unit, for example, grew from 35 people in 1976 to more than 600 in 1978.[14]

Software and Storage

Little more than two years after rolling out its first product, Amdahl was settled into its market niche. The company was interested only in large-scale computer users and sold itself based on both a superior product and seamless customer relationships rather than just hardware alone. The sales team targeted the world's largest corporations and institutions, with subsidiaries in Europe and Canada and distributors in Australia.

The company was quick to capitalize on its success with a series of product rollouts. Between 1978 and 1979, Amdahl expanded the 470 family of computers to include the V/5-II and the V/8, in addition to the original three. The top-of-the-line 470V/8 was the most advanced model available, incorporating a unique function called pre-fetching, which predicted what data would be needed and moved it from the main storage unit to the high-speed buffer for ready access. The V/8 cost between $3.3 million and $4.5 million, depending upon configuration options.

An important element of all 470 systems, and one that would become an Amdahl trademark, was that they could be upgraded in the field. This capability gave customers the opportunity to start small and expand as necessary.

Amdahl also reinforced its commitment to the original strategy of "developing a computer that would preserve the billions invested by the marketplace in applications software that ran on the industry's most common operating systems."[15] Two new software products were introduced in 1978 that enhanced the operating system of an Amdahl 470 mainframe without sacrificing its IBM compatibility.

The new Multiple Virtual Storage Systems Extension Assist (MVS/SEA) software worked in conjunction with IBM's popular MVS operating system while improving throughput approximately 12 percent.

October 1978 — Amdahl adds the 470V/8 and 470V/5-II to its offerings.

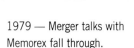

1979 — Merger talks with Memorex fall through.

September 1979 — Gene Amdahl steps down as chairman and director.

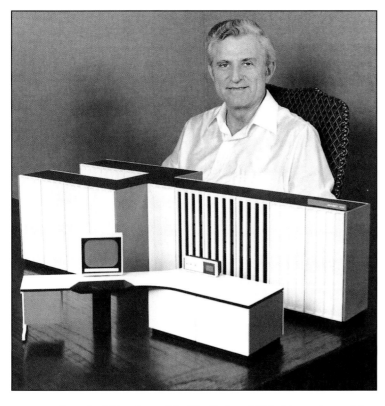

Gene Amdahl and a model of the System 470 that he made possible. In 1980, Amdahl left the company he had founded, saying it had grown too big and impersonal for him.

The Virtual Machine/Performance Enhancement (VM/PE) software package improved efficiency for customers who operated both Virtual Machine 370 (VM/370) and MVS operating systems at the same time. A year later, VM/PE Release 2.0 was introduced to allow customers to operate IBM's newly introduced Single Virtual Storage (SVS) operating system or MVS.[16]

Inside Amdahl

Before long, the three top executives found they needed to define their responsibilities in a more formal way. Until then, Amdahl and Gene White had been sharing the duties of CEO and Jack Lewis was president. The group announced a formal structure with Gene Amdahl as chairman. He would focus on future products and architecture. Gene White, the deputy chairman, would concentrate on production, financial strategy and market focus. Jack Lewis, as chief operating officer and president, remained responsible for product and engineering schedules.[17]

Amdahl was now the most successful company competing directly with IBM, though Amdahl sales

1980 — Amdahl completes and opens new 80,000-square-foot manufacturing plant near Dublin, Ireland.

1980 — Secondary public stock offering raises $54 million in new capital.

1980 — Amdahl introduces its first telecommunications product, the 4705 front-end processor.

1980 — Amdahl acquires Tran Telecommunications as a wholly owned subsidiary.

were a mere $200 million compared to IBM's $18 billion. The psychological benefits of winning the first round ran deep. Amdahl veterans recall how in those early years "there was a tremendous enthusiasm and energy and people sitting around talking about someday the stock is going to be worth $1,000 a share."[18] The company was receiving favorable press, with some media even comparing Amdahl and IBM to David and Goliath — a comparison Lewis was quick to dispel. "In David and Goliath, David kills Goliath," he said in an interview. "That was sort of a war, and the connotation isn't right. We are in the marketplace to try to bring a better product into the marketplace for customers. I think we will both win if we do it right."[19]

The growing company was also gaining a reputation as a company with a heart. Amdahl Corporation's treatment of disabled people and minorities drew particular notice. In August 1979, Amdahl was recognized as Employer of the Year by the Governor's Committee for Employment of the Handicapped for "outstanding awareness in the hiring and promotion of handicapped persons." The company also had a Woman's Network, an informal lunchtime group that offered support and direction for female employees.[20]

Despite the success of his company, by 1979 Gene Amdahl was increasingly uncomfortable at its helm. He was an entrepreneur who left IBM to escape a world of control and bureaucracy, and he craved the excitement that came with a start-up company.

In September, Amdahl announced that he was stepping down from his posts as chairman and director and from that point forward would serve only as chairman emeritus and consultant. "I do like the excitement of starting a company and operating it," Amdahl said. "What I don't like is the environment of a bureaucracy, like when I left IBM."[21] Amdahl Senior Vice President and Chief Financial Officer Clifford J. Madden left with Gene Amdahl after six years of service to Amdahl.

In an interview with the *Harvard Business Review* several months later, Amdahl reflected on the changes that had taken place at the company he had founded nine years earlier.

Fujitsu and Amdahl employees worked closely together. This 1979 photograph shows the manufacturing team for the multichip carrier.

In 1979, Amdahl installed its 200th 470V/6 system at AT&T in Youngstown, Ohio.

"The bigger it gets, the more democratic it gets. Now it might seem that a democracy ought to be a lot better than a dictatorship. Both have their weaknesses, but it's pretty hard to get the best out of a democratic procedure. What you're likely to get consensus on is unlikely to be the best in any single area. Innovation means that somebody has to do things differently, which is always painful. To be really bright, our future has to include innovation."[22]

Within a year of stepping down, Gene Amdahl relinquished his somewhat honorary posts as chairman emeritus and consultant to form a new mainframe company called Trilogy Systems. His goal was to create a giant mainframe computer that would exceed the performance of anything on the market.

Branching Out

Just before Gene Amdahl's departure, Amdahl Corporation announced in 1979 that it had entered into discussions with Memorex Corporation in hopes of merging the two companies. Memorex provided plug-compatible equipment, including tape and disk drives, processors and terminals.

"Memorex possesses a complementary product set, an excellent customer base and a strong international presence," Jack Lewis explained in a memo to all employees.[23] The plan was to merge the two companies in an exchange of stock, possibly 1.2 shares of Amdahl common stock for each common share of Memorex.

Memorex, meanwhile, was being courted by Storage Technology Corporation, a Colorado-based manufacturer of disk drives and tape drives. In the end, Memorex elected to remain independent. "While a merger with either would have created a billion-dollar computer power, financial disagreements ended both discussions," explained *Datamation* magazine.[24]

The surprising result, however, was that the two jilted suitors, Amdahl and Storage Technology Corporation, began to notice attractive qualities in each other. Negotiations between them began in early 1980. If the talks succeeded, Amdahl would become the only plug-compatible mainframe manufacturer to offer complete data processing and storage systems produced entirely in-house. Sixty percent of Amdahl's customers were already using Storage Technology's products.

Under the terms of the proposed merger, Amdahl Corporation would receive one share of the new combined company for each share given, while Storage Technology would receive three-quarters of a share for each share given. Gene White would become deputy chairman of the new company, and

Jack Lewis would become president and chief operating officer. Some marketing and maintenance operations would be consolidated.

But there was a crippling problem with the merger. Storage Technology competed directly with Amdahl benefactor Fujitsu in the disk and tape drive market, and its semiconductor plant competed with Fujitsu in that same market.[25] Storage Technology Corporation's potential intimacy with Amdahl Corporation made Fujitsu management nervous. Fujitsu, which held three out of eight seats on Amdahl's board of directors, wanted to clarify and modify some of the licensing agreements between Amdahl and Storage Technology Corporation. Executives at Storage Technology Corporation balked. Explained Gene White:

"Fujitsu and Amdahl have complex and comprehensive agreements covering cross-licensing of certain future technologies.... STC would not agree to

the requested modifications, and, accordingly, STC and Amdahl terminated the merger agreement."[26]

The collapse of the STC deal did not stifle Amdahl's desire to diversify. Amdahl officials announced in 1980 that the company would acquire Tran Telecommunications as a wholly owned subsidiary. Based in Marina Del Rey, California, Tran Telecommunications designed and manufactured digital switches and concentrators that connected various kinds of hardware to a central network. In 1979, Tran posted revenues of $22 million and employed more than 400 people.[27] The acquisition was completed before the end of the year.[28]

The acquisition had an immediate positive side effect: the introduction of the Model 4705 Programmable Communications Processor.[29] The 4705 provided an interface between large mainframes and their communications network.[30]

At the 1979 stockholders' meeting, Amdahl's officers were able to report on the successful 470 line of machines and the company's growing product line.

Like other Amdahl products, the 4705 offered better performance than competitive products at a lower price. Also, capitalizing on a traditional Amdahl approach, the product was compatible with its IBM counterpart, the 3705-II front-end processor, though costing 10 to 15 percent less and offering 1.8 times the capacity.

Good Publicity

With the acquisition complete, Amdahl received some unexpected good publicity from its chief competitor. During a protracted IBM antitrust trial, IBM introduced confidential documents that compared its products to seven Amdahl Corporation processors. Of the seven Amdahl systems, five were considered superior to the IBM counterpart.[31]

Overall, 1980 was a good year for Amdahl. The company completed its 80,000-square-foot facility in Ireland and added new training centers.

A stock issue in the latter part of the year resulted in $54 million in proceeds, which coupled with strong sales to help Amdahl finish the year with a cash balance of $83 million.[32] Total revenue for 1980 was $394.3 million, a 23 percent increase over 1979. Net income had declined 1 percent, to $15.2 million. By the end of 1980, Amdahl Corporation had grown to more than 4,000 full-time employees.[33]

Throughout this period, Amdahl continued to offer upgrades and improvements to its 470 series. The 470V/7A, introduced in late 1979, greatly increased the capacity of a V/7 or V/8, as well as the performance of a V/5 and V/5-II.[34] Toward the end of 1980, Amdahl introduced the 470V/7C. With 45 percent of the power of a standard V/7, the new machine was aimed at the entry-level market.[35]

In those early years, Amdahl was singularly committed to growth within the mainframe market. The company had been founded to produce a better mainframe, and any acquisitions or ventures were planned with that in mind. But the acquisition of Tran communications and Amdahl's entry into networking technologies would prove to have lasting consequences as the company later moved toward becoming a complete data processing technology company. In response to a reporter's question about Amdahl's position in the industry and future, Gene White, deputy chairman, was clearly optimistic.

"Many people ask us the question, 'How will Amdahl Corporation direct its orientation toward the marketplace?' The answer to that question is that the opportunity in the total market we address is far greater than any incremental opportunity, and the demands from that growth take all the management's time and attention."[36]

Amdahl, led by President Jack Lewis and CEO and Chairman Gene White, was anxious to score again when it announced the next generation of plug-compatible mainframe computers in 1980. Tension and excitement across the entire industry ran high. "Everybody agreed that we had done an outstanding job with the 470 and its various forms, recalled Sales Manager Tony DeMory. "The question was, could we do it a second time?"[37]

In the early eighties, Amdahl began to diversify its product offerings. This operator is using a 580 enhanced with Amdahl storage devices.

CHAPTER SIX

THE NEXT GENERATION
1981–1984

"I think we started believing a little too much of our own hype. A machine that we said would be cheap and faster did end up being less expensive, but it was disastrously late and terribly unreliable."

— Sales Manager Tony DeMory[1]

THE STORY OF THE MUCH-anticipated 580 series begins with an announcement by IBM. On November 12, 1980, IBM announced its next generation of large-scale systems, code-named "H" or "Hickory." These systems featured the Model 3081 processor with double the performance of the company's flagship 3033 model. The system, according to IBM marketing hype, would be difficult to replicate because its instructions, or "microcoding," were built into system components rather than supplied through software.[2] The price would range between $4 million and $4.6 million.[3]

Industry observers did not have to wait long for Amdahl's response.

Six days later, Amdahl announced its own new line of mainframes, the 580 series, which would be "a logical extension of the innovative design and technology used in 470 series large-scale systems."[4] Featuring Amdahl's trademark LSI circuitry, the 580 family initially consisted of the 5860 single processor and the 5880 multi-processor mainframes.

The 5860, which was supposed to be rolled out in early 1982, offered twice the performance of the 470V/8, while the 5880 was predicted to be 3.5 times more powerful.[5] Furthermore, the 5860 was expected to occupy only 55 square feet of floor space, one-third less than the V/8.[6]

Although superior in performance, the 580 series built on the successful design of the 470 machine. Like the 470, the powerful new computers were air-cooled. They were, however, capable of packing 400 circuits on a single chip, which was four times the number of circuits on a 470 chip and hopefully translated into better performance and reliability. The working heart of the computer was the Multiple Chip Carrier, which was designed to carry several LSI chip packages on a single, field-replaceable board. Each MCC board contained 121 memory and logic integrated-circuit chips. Each system had between eight and 13 MCC boards.[7] By stacking the boards on top of one another, connection distances were shortened further, again resulting in increased speed.[8]

To ensure that the system would be compatible with IBM's architecture, Amdahl developed macrocode, or software that ran on top of the hardware. "We were convinced that we could put this fairly simple piece of software on top of the hard-

These towers, mounted on 580 chip packages, dissipated heat generated by the system's dense circuitry.

ware and that would enable us to quickly respond to architectural changes made by IBM," said Dave Brewer, an engineering manager on the project who later served as vice president of processor products.[9]

Multiple Domain Feature

Another revolutionary capability was planned for later models of the 580 series: the Multiple Domain Feature (MDF). This feature allowed processors to use different operating systems simultaneously. It saved customers a great deal of money by allowing them to divide a single processor's capacity among several individual tasks with completely autonomous programs. With this feature, an experimental application could also be tested on a system without having to interrupt its regular production workload.[10]

And most importantly, it was a feature that IBM could not offer. "It was such a powerful capability, and we had it for three and a half or four years before IBM had it," said Allen Buskirk, an engineer who joined Amdahl right out of Brigham Young University in 1971.[11]

President Jack Lewis recalled that it was hard to convince customers that the revolutionary prod-

uct would work, but the effort was worth it. The Multiple Domain Feature was unique. "It ended up being a major differentiator for us and changed the architecture of large-scale systems for a long time," he said.[12]

In October 1981, Amdahl announced that another model, the 5870, would be added to the 580 series by the end of 1983. With an additional processing unit, the 5870 would have 70 percent more power than the 5860. Its price ranged from $5.4 million to $6.1 million.[13]

Software Products

That same year, Amdahl also introduced the UTS system, which allowed mainframe users to work in a Unix environment. Unix was a relatively new operating system that was attracting significant numbers of small system users. Created by Bell Labs in 1969, Unix was a flexible, open operating system. Amdahl's UTS allowed companies with Unix applications to run them in a mainframe environment, providing enhanced scalability and availability.[14]

The UTS system gained popularity quickly, its market exposure enhanced by several marketing agreements between Amdahl and other compa-

1981 — Amdahl introduces the UTS system.

October 1981 — Amdahl announces plans to add the high-end Model 5870 to its 580 family of computers.

May 1982 — Amdahl creates the Peripheral Products Division and introduces data Storage Systems.

nies.[15] One such arrangement took place two years later when California-based Relational Technology, Inc., agreed to market its INGRES database management system under Amdahl's UTS-Unix operating system.[16] Later agreements with Oracle for its relational database management system and with Bellcore for telecommunications applications also gave the UTS business a boost.

According to *Datamation* magazine, Amdahl's movement into the Unix environment was positioning the company to realize long-range benefits.

"As if to show that it does not merely react to announcements made by IBM, Amdahl was perhaps the first company to support Unix on a mainframe.... Unix was ported to an Amdahl system and, in 1980, emerged as an Amdahl product called UTS. It's the kind of product that can get a company like Amdahl into new accounts, a prospect that is far from unattractive."[17]

Ready for Launch

Throughout 1982, anticipation continued to build for the 580 launch, which was expected any

The hoses jutting out of this 580 were used to test specific environmental factors.

August 1982 — The day of the first Model 5860 shipment, Amdahl's stock rises from $18 to $27. The computers are found to be unreliable, and engineers begin working feverishly to correct the problems.

1983 — Amdahl forms the Communications Systems Division; the company debuts on the *Fortune* 500 list at position 469.

December 1982 — First problem-free Model 5860 is installed.

May 1983 — Gene White steps down as chief executive officer and is succeeded by Jack Lewis.

A technician affixes a 580 label to a system before it is shipped out.

month. CEO Gene White even went so far as to tell reporters that the 580 would be the featured Amdahl product, with no substantial changes, into the mid-1980s.[18]

Even before the launch, however, pressure was building around the machine. IBM, which had been at the center of a Justice Department antitrust suit, was cleared of all charges and aggressively pursued its smaller competitor, slashing prices by 10 to 15 percent annually. Beginning in 1979, Big Blue also began rolling out new products regularly, causing many of Amdahl's customers to lease instead of buy.

An article in *Financial World* noted how critical the 580 line was to Amdahl.

"Amdahl's future depends almost entirely on the success of its new 580 line — especially with sales and profits on the older 470 line trailing off. The big question is whether IBM can muscle Amdahl. Despite some worries about the 'surprises' that IBM could pull, the consensus of about

a dozen top computer analysts is that Amdahl can take the heat from IBM."[19]

Investment in the 580 series of products ran into the hundreds of millions of dollars. To help fund development, Amdahl replaced its previous $260 million credit line with $370 million procured through an unsecured revolving credit agreement with 12 international banks.[20] The stakes were continuing to rise.

To prepare for a major sales and marketing initiative, Joseph J. Francesconi and Daniel W. Tierney were promoted to corporate vice presidents early in 1982. These Amdahl veterans brought valuable experience in marketing and product support services to the company's executive leadership.[21] Former Senior Vice President of United States operations Ken Simonds was promoted to executive vice president, filling a new position that would be responsible for domestic product and service support, marketing, software, manufacturing, operations and documentation.[22]

Amdahl's corporate culture was becoming more formal and efficient.

"When I arrived at Amdahl in 1981, it was obvious to me that something had to be done fast," said John Adler, then vice president in charge of engineering and product development. Adler, who joined IBM in 1960, had previously come into contact with Gene Amdahl when Amdahl was director of IBM's Los Gatos Development Lab. "Fast," however, was not necessarily yet part of the corporate culture:

"For example, when I would call a staff meeting, nobody would show up on time. So, I dialed up the recorded time announcement on the phone and put it on the public address system so everyone would know just how late they were. It worked. Everyone started coming to meetings on time. It was the beginning of an 'on-time culture' at Amdahl, and I think it was successfully carried over into the development process."[23]

Larry Boucher of Adaptec lured Adler away from Amdahl in May 1985. In 1996, Adler was chairman of the nearly $1 billion hardware and software company, which specializes in the elimination of performance bottlenecks between computers, peripherals and networks.

A Valuable Disaster

In August 1982, the company delivered its first 5860. Unfortunately, the machine was already late to market due to complications in the design. Regardless of its tardiness, the company's solid reputation inspired confidence in the investment community. The day of the shipment, the company's shares on the American Stock Exchange rose 50 percent, from $18 to $27.[24] By the fourth quarter of 1982, Amdahl had already recorded orders for 20 systems.[25]

Unfortunately for Amdahl, however, the 5860 did not live up to expectations. Customers, who had learned to expect better performance from mainframes, began to report reliability problems that could be traced to the 580's complicated new design. In some cases, the system's performance was about 60 percent below what had been promised.

"It was an unmitigated disaster," remembered Adler. He was later put in charge of developing its successor, the 5890 series of mainframes, codenamed Apache, in which Amdahl avoided the problems with the 580 series. "The crisis was real, and real evident," Adler said. "The MTBF (mean-time between failures) of our 580 was an appallingly

Amdahl's new generation of computers, the 580 series, had some difficulties at first but eventually became a popular product line for the company.

short 180 hours, versus IBM's 4,000 hours. We clearly had our work cut out for us."[26]

"I think we started believing a little too much of our own hype," said Sales Manager Tony DeMory. "A machine that we said would be cheaper and faster did end up being less expensive, but it was disastrously late and terribly unreliable. One of the first users of the 5860 was Michigan Bell in Detroit. Unfortunately, it was my account. They were so upset that they literally unplugged the machine."[27]

There were many problems. The machine had a new chip technology and a new design architecture, and a new automated design system had been used to develop it. "Too many things changed all at once," said Dave Chambers, project manager for the design part of the team that was called in to fix the machine.[28]

The problems with the 580 series, according to Dave Brewer, an engineer who led the task force to improve performance, could be traced to two basic causes: unrealistic design specifications imposed by Gene Amdahl and a development team that was behind the curve set by IBM regarding product reliability.

While the 580 was still in development, Gene Amdahl decided he wanted to address the cache memory of the 580 series with virtual addresses instead of converting the virtual addresses to real addresses before going to the cache. Like many of Amdahl's ideas, this was a radical departure from anything done at the time, and it was possibly beyond the reach of the engineers.

As it turned out, Amdahl engineers spent nine critical months in development working to design the complex system — and even then the first performance testing fell short of the team's goals. Brewer remembered when the engineering team first realized there was serious trouble with the system:

"I'll never forget the phone call I got one evening. Mike Clements, chief technology officer, called when the first performance testing was done on the engineering model. Based on the performance architecture modeling, we were expecting 1.8 to 2 times the V8's performance, and what we got instead was 1.1. Everybody's first reaction was, 'Oh, there must be a miswire somewhere. When we find it and fix it, performance will be OK.' But it wasn't. It took months of incremental improvement in all parts of the system to get the performance up to 1.78 times the V8, the goal we set for ourselves. We used up all the tricks we would have liked to save for a performance upgrade midway through the product life. We never did find the smoking gun in the cache system that explained the problem."[29]

Even with the upgraded machine, customers were still unhappy. But the seriousness of the reliability problems had less to do with the 580 than with the customers themselves, who had come to expect better performance. When Amdahl introduced the 470 system, the company had set a new

An operator at the terminal of a 580 system.

benchmark for reliability in mainframes. At the time, it was acceptable to work out problems in the early installations after the machine was up and running at a customer site.

With the 580, Amdahl engineers expected the same leeway — customers who were willing to let the company correct problems after the machine had been installed. But IBM, using the 470 as a "motivator," had raised the bar. Big Blue initiated an elaborate in-house testing program and rigorously tested its first machines before sending them out, meaning the first installations were no longer plagued by reliability problems.

Compared with the 470 introduction, the 580's reliability problems were about average. But when compared to IBM, the 580 appeared to be a terribly unreliable machine and customers were immediately incensed about problems in the already-late machine.

Working Day and Night

Even the most frustrated customers recognized that Amdahl was committed to solving the problems. "Every customer who has ever dealt with us will tell you that, however disappointed they were or how hard it got, we always fixed whatever we said we were going to fix," DeMory said. "Always. No matter what it cost us."[30] As always, a customer's problem was an Amdahl problem.

A team of about 60 engineers worked night and day to iron out the system's flaws. "There was a real sense of teamwork and a lot of communication between the design engineers and myself and the production people," Brewer said. In a mere four months, the team increased the system's performance by 60 percent.[31] John Matthews, who was in support service at the time, remembered the atmosphere of teamwork across Amdahl:

"We started having meetings every Thursday afternoon, and Jack Lewis was there, and he's a little bit of a technician himself. He would run the meetings, and basically what we did is we'd look at all the problems we had the previous week and say, 'This is a power problem. This is a buffer problem, etc.' We'd look for trends so we could see where we needed to put the energy. Lewis would get us in there on Thursday and

beat on engineering until they came up with a fix, and then he'd beat on me until we got the fix put on in the field. It was a slow, gradual improvement on reliability."[32]

Amdahl engineers went to extraordinary lengths to solve the glitches with as little inconvenience to customers as possible. For example, the Bank of Montreal could not shut down the system to allow engineers enough time to diagnose a problem and find a solution. So Amdahl had to recreate the bank's data center, said William Ferone, a customer service veteran since 1978 who eventually became vice president of customer service.

"Obviously, we didn't get 87 IBM machines, but we brought in some of our other CPUs from our own data center. We brought over some used machines that we were selling. We put some storage together. Brought in a test system that was very close to what we thought they were running. They even gave us some of their production workload. So we were pretty close to simulating their environment. We worked for about three days, building as close to a mirror image as possible of the part of their data center that was having the problem, and we wound up recreating the problem."[33]

Amdahl spent millions of dollars fixing the problems with the 580 — and customers stuck with the company. "We had a lot of customer loyalty from the 470 days, plus they wanted to take care of themselves by keeping IBM's competition alive; they stuck with us," Matthews said.[34]

Recovery

With the problems beginning to recede, the company announced in September 1982 that it was planning on shipping the first 5880 in early 1983 and that it was adding another model to the line. The entry-level 5850, priced at $2.75 million, would fill the gap between the high-performance 470V/8 and the more powerful 5860.[35]

Nevertheless, Amdahl still had to reassure the financial community of the market potential of the 580 series. In November, San Francisco Bay Area security analysts peppered Gene White with questions about the shipping delays. "The reasons for the delay are behind us," White responded. "The solutions are either in place or will be in place this quarter." He also announced that the still-popular 470V/8 would be taken out of production by the middle of 1983 to make way for the new system.[36] The following month, in December 1982, Amdahl installed its first problem-free 5860, finally achieving what the company had hoped to accomplish before the system was originally scheduled to be shipped months before.[37]

Despite annual revenues in 1982 of $462.2 million, which represented a 4 percent increase over 1981, high startup costs, unfavorable currency exchange rates and the delay in 5860 shipments resulted in a 75 percent drop in annual net income. However, both income and revenue began to rebound in the fourth quarter, and executives were confident that the trend would continue in the new year since the glitches in the 580 had been worked out.[38]

"Financially, it was quite tough," recalled Michael B. Shahbazian, who was assistant treasurer at the time. Shahbazian had joined Amdahl in 1979 and moved through the financial ranks to become vice president and treasurer in 1989. "We had a strong 1981, and we thought we were well-positioned for an extremely strong 1982 with a new product coming out. We found ourselves really scrambling to recover."[39]

Many Amdahl customers used the new 580 series (right) alongside the older 470 models (left) to meet their data processing needs.

The first two models in the 6000 storage system series were the Model 6880 Storage Control Unit (left) and the 6280 Disk Storage Unit (right).

Reflecting on the tumultuous year, President Jack Lewis summarized his feelings by quoting the character Linus from the Peanuts cartoon strip: "There is no heavier burden than a great potential."[40]

6000 Series Storage Systems

Although the most critical development of the year was the 580, Amdahl was not too consumed by its mainframes to continue diversifying into other aspects of large-scale computing. In May 1982, Amdahl created the Peripheral Products Division, which would provide disk drives and controllers used to centrally store information. The new division was led by Stephen S. Smith, former vice president of business planning.[41]

The division introduced its first product in September — the 6000 series storage system, described by CEO Gene White as "a complement to our principal strategic products, the central processing units."[42] This was followed by the 6380 and 6380E storage products over the next two years.

Shortly after Amdahl entered the storage market, an independent research group known as Reliability Plus gave the 6380 its highest rating in the large-disk storage market category by a margin of more than two to one. "The reliability of the 6000 series is proving to be better than advertised," said Ed LeClair, the manager of customer

service at Software Pursuits, one of Amdahl's early storage customers.[43] More than 150 subsystems were sold by the end of the year.

The New Year Begins

By early 1983, the earlier difficulties with the 5860 had been resolved, and sales of the system were strong. In the first three months of the year, 35 systems were shipped.[44] In order to meet the high demand, the manufacturing plant in Swords, Ireland, began manufacturing 580s that spring.[45]

In August 1983, however, Amdahl announced that engineering problems had developed with the 5880, and its scheduled launch would be pushed back. Wall Street reacted with apprehension, but Amdahl Chairman Gene White brushed aside concerns by emphasizing the already proven success of the 580 series and Amdahl's developing focus on software and peripherals. "We've got a lot more up our sleeves than this one box," he told a reporter.[46]

Amdahl had learned a hard lesson with the launch of the 580 series and was moving in several directions at once. The company was pouring more than $100 million annually into research and development, about 30 percent of which supported products other than Amdahl mainframes.[47] The new product mix featured high-volume data storage devices, network and communications products, software, and educational services. Meanwhile, new 580s were rolled out, including the 5840 and 5870, each geared to different needs within the mainframe market.

Communications Systems

Diversification continued as Amdahl pushed further into communications systems, a trend that started with the Tran Telecommunications acquisition. Almost simultaneously in 1983, the company created the Communications Systems Division in Marina del Rey, California, and introduced a new line of products, beginning with the February 1983 introduction of the 2211 series Time Division Multiplexer.

Two months later, Amdahl introduced the 4705E Communications Processor, an enhanced version of the 3-year-old 4705 Communications

Above: Amdahl's product line in the early eighties. From left to right: a Model 6880 Storage Control Unit, a Model 6280 Disk Storage Unit, a System 580 and a 4705 Programmable Communications Processor.

Below: As part of its commitment to training customers, Amdahl published software manuals such as these.

Processor. Amdahl communications processors allowed users to mix voice, video and data from multiple sources over a network. The 4705E offered 35 percent more power than the 4705 and was compatible with IBM's Systems Network Architecture (SNA). Even better, it did not require the user to convert software during memory upgrades, a necessity for users of IBM's 3725 processor.[48]

The 4470 Network Concentrator, introduced in December 1983, was a packet assembly/disassembly device that allowed a central processor to understand and reconstitute files that had been bundled into digital packets for transmission across a network. The 4705 Communications Processor and follow-on models became the most successful of Amdahl's communications products.

Education

As its technologies became more demanding, Amdahl moved into education and training to further help customers understand its products and best use them in a large-scale data processing environment. This focus was nothing new — Amdahl had committed itself to superior customer service and training since the introduction of its first product. As a result of this commitment, by the early 1980s, the company was among the nation's leading systems software and program-

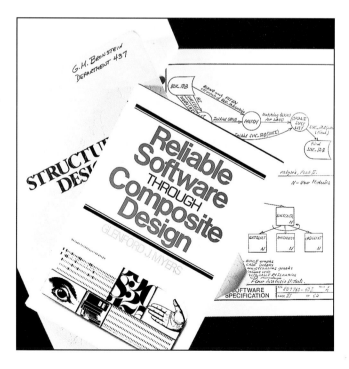

Above: While retaining the title of president, Jack Lewis was promoted to chief executive officer in 1983.

Right: Edward F. Thompson became vice president, chief financial officer and secretary of Amdahl in 1983.

ming educators. Classes were organized through the Education and Professional Services Division in the United States, Canada and Europe.

The Amdahl Phenomenon

By this time, the company operated in more than 20 countries and worked with the world's most demanding customers, including AT&T and the United States Postal Service. These customers required more than a powerful processor — they wanted complete solutions to their information-processing needs. By offering networking and communications products, storage, and educational support, Amdahl was steadily evolving into a full-service solution company. Its efforts were rewarded, and in 1983, a growing Amdahl

first achieved *Fortune* 500 status with a ranking of 469.[49]

Also in 1983, Gene White stepped down from his post as chief executive officer and was succeeded by Jack Lewis, who continued to serve as president and chief operating officer. White retained his position as chairman of the board.[50] Later in the year, Edward F. Thompson was promoted from vice president and treasurer to vice president, chief financial officer and secretary. Thompson had been given the opportunity to serve as chief financial officer of Gene Amdahl's new company, Trilogy Systems, but had elected to remain at Amdahl.[51]

As the new corporate officers settled into their positions, Amdahl launched a promotional campaign called the Amdahl Phenomenon. Its goal was to double the growth rate of the company's customer base — from 15 percent to 30 percent. New product offerings, enhanced customer service and education, and sales to established customers were elements of the campaign.[52]

According to Lewis, this inaugural image advertising campaign would "reinforce the leadership position that we have achieved."[53]

In its history, Amdahl had never indulged in aggressive mass-market advertising. Amdahl veteran Henry Cassel explained that the company didn't need flashy print or television advertisements. With a small group of less than 1,500 customers, word of mouth was Amdahl's most valuable asset. "The reason is," Cassel noted, "the people who need to know who Amdahl is already know who Amdahl is."[54]

But this advertising strategy paid off. It helped Amdahl win such important assignments as a $21 million contract with the Australian Department of Social Security to install Amdahl systems at the Australian National Computer Center.[55] The contract, announced in June 1983, was part of a $100 million plan by the Australian government to update the Department of Social Security's data processing services.[56] When completed, it would be one of the largest civilian data processing networks outside the United States.[57] With Amdahl's strong showing in Australia, the company could move deeper into the Pacific Basin region by the end of the year, opening offices in Singapore, Hong Kong and New Zealand.[58]

Expanding the 580 Series

Even as Amdahl's product lineup diversified, the 580 series remained the company's most important product line. In mid-June 1983, Amdahl announced the Model 5840. Slated for introduction by the end of the year, it would cost $2.35 million and offer 55 to 65 percent of the performance of the 5860.[59]

The company also announced that it would modify its 470 and 580 series of mainframe computers to support IBM's MVS/XA (Extended Architecture) operating system, which had emerged as a new industry software standard. That support would not be available until the middle of 1984.[60] IBM had introduced Extended Architecture in April,[61] and to fill the gap, Amdahl introduced the MVS/XA/Conversion Assist Feature, which enabled two separate operating systems, such as MVS/370 and MVS/XA, to function within the same environment.[62]

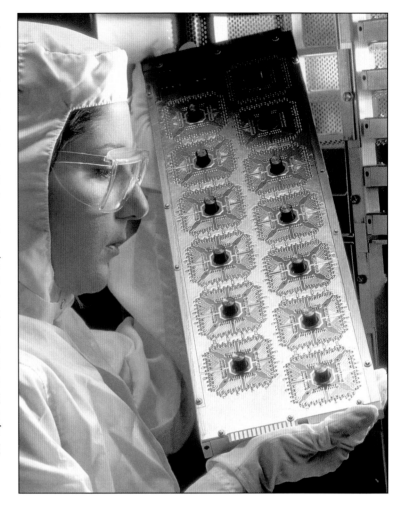

Amdahl's second generation of computers, the 580 series, used Multiple Chip Carriers that united circuits and memory on the same board. The board is shown being placed in a chamber that utilized power and temperature to extend the life of the chips.

In July 1984, Hydro Quebec became one of the first users of the Model 5860 uniprocessor with MVS/XA support. Hydro Quebec, the only electric utility company in the enormous Canadian province, was able to transfer four information management systems to the lone Model 5860 using multiple domains — a task its IBM 3033s could not accomplish.[63] By the middle of 1984, almost 300 systems of the 580 series had been sold.[64]

Thanks to the success of the 580, revenue for 1983 shot up 68 percent, to $777.7 million. All the development costs of the previous year were paid, so income jumped 587 percent, to $46.5 million.

Amdahl closed 1983 with 6,600 employees and a worldwide installed base of approximately 950 mainframe systems.[65]

Early in 1984, Amdahl announced that it was adding two more models to the 580 series. The 5867 Dual Processor and 5868 Multiprocessor filled the performance gap between the 5860 and 5880.[66] Customers could easily upgrade the models to their more powerful counterparts. Priced between $3.4 million and $4.1 million, they would be available by fall.[67]

A smaller product, the 580/Accelerator, was available early in the year. This $3,000 item, another industry first for Amdahl, offered owners of Model 5840 and 5850 machines the ability to access more processing power during periods of peak demand.[68]

Customer loyalty to Amdahl continued to grow, and 30 percent of Amdahl's customers claimed to be Amdahl-only shops.[69] In a survey of 3,000 computer users nationwide, Amdahl was rated second in overall excellence. IBM placed fourth.[70]

Fujitsu's Growing Influence

In May 1984, the Heizer Corporation, the investment firm that had helped Gene Amdahl get off the ground in 1970, sold 18 percent of its 20 percent share of the company to Fujitsu, Limited. The deal was prompted by a change in tax law, said E.F. Heizer, Jr., "Otherwise, we wouldn't have sold it."[71]

The transaction increased Fujitsu's holdings from slightly more than 30 percent to 49 percent, leading the press to speculate about the powerful company's role in Amdahl operations. Fujitsu executives, however, did not interfere with day-to-day management.[72] "They never tried to use their ownership to push the company down a given path," said Chairman Gene White. "They let the company make its own decisions."[73]

A Joint Standing Committee was formed with the top three executives at Amdahl and the top three at Fujitsu. "The idea was that they would meet twice a year and just discuss everything," said Bert O'Neill, Amdahl's secretary for those meetings. To help foster cross-cultural understanding, O'Neill and his Japanese counterpart, a Mr. Urano, would take each other to dinner on occasion. It took O'Neill a while to learn about the difference between Japanese and American customs. O'Neill said on one occasion he invited Mr. Urano and his wife to dinner at his house.

"You know, as an American it's the natural thing to do. So the first time I asked, he said his wife couldn't make it because his daughter broke her arm. The next time, something else happened and his wife couldn't make it. Eventually it got through my thick skull. This was just the Japanese way of saying 'no.' It is the way the Japanese do things. They don't involve their wives in business."[74]

O'Neill went on to teach courses in Japanese culture so other Amdahl employees wouldn't make the same mistakes he had.

An Uphill Battle

Stagnant income in the second quarter of 1984 forced the company to lay off 300 of its 7,200 employees.[75] Among the root causes of the decline in sales was the increasingly strong dollar, which hurt the company's exports because 40 percent of the company's business came from overseas.[76]

Another challenge came from IBM, which adopted a new strategy of delaying the release of technical information about upcoming products, said Greg Handschuh, vice president of legal affairs.

To remain both competitive and compatible, Amdahl studied IBM's product specifications as published in the *IBM Principles of Operations Manual.* After buying IBM's processor, technicians would examine its documentation and test it extensively by monitoring the system's response to specific instructions.

In an effort to prevent Amdahl and other IBM-compatible manufacturers from reproducing or improving on the IBM design, IBM began withholding source code and other vital information about its systems until after new products had been shipped.

Amdahl had filed a complaint with the European Commission in the late seventies arguing against IBM's practice of delaying disclosure of such information, which was critical to the success of plug-compatible manufacturers like Amdahl. In most cases, a company is not under obligation to publish such information unless withholding the information gives the company a monopoly advantage. After five years of investigation, during which even the U.S. government tried to persuade the Commission to drop the case, the Commission was ready to issue a formal complaint. "At that time, IBM made a proposal which has since come to be known as the 'Undertaking,'" said Handschuh. "They voluntarily agreed to make the information available within 120 days of product announcement at the latest, but in no event later than the first customer shipment." This agreement remained in effect until 1995.[77]

But other changes at IBM presented more difficulties for Amdahl. Competition had forced IBM to offer better products at lower prices. Since 1975,

prices had plummeted, and cycle time required to develop and introduce next-generation computers dropped from seven years to only four. Meanwhile, the cost of developing new generations of computers had increased tenfold.[78] The explosive personal computer and minicomputer market also created new challenges for plug-compatible mainframe manufacturers, who watched their large-scale products decline in popularity as customers began experimenting with the smaller, less expensive systems.[79]

Amdahl entered the supercomputer market in 1984 with two models manufactured by Fujitsu. However, the business never really caught on.

Some computer companies looked at the tightening market and elected to withdraw from the field. One of Amdahl's competitors, National Advanced Systems, stopped manufacturing mainframes altogether and became a distributor for Hitachi. Storage Technology Corporation terminated plans to build an IBM-compatible system in February, and Magnuson had liquidated its inventory a year earlier.[80]

Amdahl reviewed its market strategy and forecasts and decided to continue diversification. In September 1984, Amdahl announced plans to enter the supercomputer market distributing two of Fujitsu's systems.[81] These large, ultra-powerful systems were intended for scientific applications. Unfortunately, "Buy American" policies of major government and university users kept them from purchasing Japanese supercomputers, and

Amdahl sold only about a dozen units, almost exclusively in Europe.

Amdahl reported revenue of $779.4 million for 1984 — only $1.7 million more than 1983. Net income dropped 22 percent to $36.4 million.[82] Yet the company remained committed to research and development, spending 16.3 percent of revenues, or $129.9 million, on developing and improving its products.[83]

Jack Lewis' annual message to shareholders emphasized Amdahl's confidence in the future of its markets:

"The expansion and scope of our product offerings — central processors, storage products, communications products and software — encompass some of the highest growth segments in the data processing industry."[84]

The circuit board of the 5890 series, introduced by Amdahl in 1985.

CHAPTER SEVEN

NEW PRODUCTS AND NEW OPPORTUNITIES

1985–1986

"The stronger IBM gets, the better our opportunity. People are going to start looking at IBM's market share and question the wisdom of it. We are poised to take advantage of this."

— Amdahl COO Joe Zemke, 1985[1]

IN 1985 AND 1986, AMDAHL'S business would follow the now-familiar pattern of a new product launch, a period of market acceptance and then booming sales. In this case, Amdahl scored with a new generation of high-end processors, the 5890 series. Meanwhile, the company continued to build its other product lines and diversify within the realm of large-scale information processing. It was a good time to celebrate Amdahl's 15th anniversary. By then, Amdahl could no longer claim to be a struggling upstart with one great product. It was a global company with a good reputation and a cohesive line of strong products.

E. Joseph Zemke

The company's directors made a far-reaching decision in May 1985. E. Joseph Zemke was hired as chief operating officer, filling a position that had been vacant since Jack Lewis had become CEO two years earlier. Zemke had been with IBM for nearly 20 years and had most recently been the chief executive officer of Auto-Trol Technology Corporation, a computer and design firm based in Denver, Colorado.[2] With annual sales of $75 million, Auto-Trol was much smaller than Amdahl. But Lewis, who was starting to think about who would succeed him at the helm of the company, liked Zemke's background.

"The fact that I was CEO of a small company was attractive to him," noted Zemke.

"But even more attractive was that I had almost 20 years at IBM. I had built a good reputation for understanding large computers. In the process of being at Auto-Trol for five years, I had gotten rounded out a little more about investors and engineering and all kinds of things. I was attracted because it was the next logical step and I really liked the people at Amdahl."[3]

Zemke was responsible for day-to-day management while Lewis focused on long-term strategies.[4] The company reorganized its manufacturing and engineering operations, placing both under the direction of Bruce O. Beebe. Responsibility for CPU product development was given to former 580 systems manager David Brewer.[5] Both had been hired on the same day in 1970 and had shared an office while working for IBM during the early 1960s.[6] Together, Brewer and Beebe worked to maintain the team atmosphere that had propelled Amdahl to its current level of prominence.

The 5890 mainframe. Code-named Apache, the 5890 series would be among the most popular in Amdahl history.

An aerial view of Amdahl's main campus in Sunnyvale, taken in 1985.

1984 — European headquarters established at the Dogmersfield Park estate in England.

May 1985 — E. Joseph Zemke is hired as chief operating officer.

1985 — Amdahl begins construction that will double manufacturing capacity of its plant in Ireland.

As in its earliest days, Amdahl was determined to hire bright people, work them hard and reward them well.

Regaining Market Share

The challenges the company faced followed almost immediately. In the first months of 1985, Amdahl was confronted with a disturbing fact. Over the previous 12 months, the company's market share of installed mainframes had declined from 10 percent to 8 percent, while IBM saw a 3 percent increase, giving the larger firm almost 90 percent of the domestic mainframe market.[7]

A small step toward better penetration of its markets was to enter into a series of marketing agreements that gained Amdahl access to outside distribution networks.

The company signed an agreement to promote UTS, which had been introduced in 1981 as the world's first UNIX-based operating system for System 390 mainframes. Software developer Oracle Corporation agreed to distribute its relational data base management system to more than 750 installations under Amdahl's UTS operating system.[8]

The Bread and Butter

But Amdahl's real focus on profitability was through the 580 family of mainframes, which had finally gained market acceptance. "We had very good shipments between 1984 and 1986," recalled Mike Shahbazian, the company treasurer. "I don't think anybody realized it until the end because it was a product that always carried a taint with it."[9]

To meet production demands for the seven models available in the 580 series, Amdahl announced a major expansion of its manufacturing plant in Swords, Ireland, which was producing 40 percent of all Amdahl mainframes. The expansion, scheduled to be completed in 1988, called for doubling the manufacturing space from 78,000 square feet to 159,000 square feet and increasing the staff from 350 employees to 550. Ireland's Industrial Development Authority provided a grant that would cover 20 percent of the cost.[10]

The 5890 Series

Then in late 1985, Amdahl made the announcement that would govern its welfare for the next few years. The 5890 series, code-named Apache, was

October 1985 — The 5890 series of mainframe computers is announced.

April 1986 — Amdahl announces the 6680 Electronic Direct Access Storage device.

June 1986 — The first 5890 mainframe is shipped to Southland Corporation in Dallas.

January 1986 — The UTS/580 is introduced.

unveiled as the company's newest and most powerful mainframe yet. Positioned at the very high end of any mainframes on the market, the 5890 line initially consisted of three models: the 5890-200 dual processor with degraded performance, the 5890-300 full-performance dual processor and the 5890-600 four-way multiprocessor. The 5890-180 and 5890-190 uniprocessors, the 5890-390 two-way multiprocessor and the 5890-400 three-way multiprocessor were added to the series in 1987 and 1988. Dave Chambers, who started working with Amdahl straight out of Stanford University in 1972, was called in to direct the project. He had helped troubleshoot the 580 once problems arose, and he was trusted to bring the new mainframes to market. Prior to his retirement in 1998, he headed up engineering and development for all of Amdahl's hardware products. Chambers remembers the 5890 era fondly:

"I am very proud of the 5890, and I think the team that worked on it is very proud as well. It shipped on schedule in June of 1986 and exceeded the performance goal. It also set the standard for reliability in the industry. My role was to come in and make sure it was organized. Because of my experience on the 580, I understood what it took to get the project out. The good thing for me was there was this absolutely manic group of people dedicated to making this a great project."[11]

The development of the 5890 dated to 1981, when Amdahl engineers began discussing what the next generation of chips would look like. By the middle of 1982, the development teams had mapped out the 5890's overall design. Over the next years, hundreds of Amdahl employees were involved. Logic designers developed the chip's design, a design automation group translated the logical chip designs into physical semiconductor designs, and mechanical engineers produced the packaging designs.

Throughout the development stages, Amdahl engineers drew on the lessons they learned with the problematic 580s. They limited the number of new variables in the upgraded product. Engineer Allen Buskirk explained that the 5890 simply expanded on the technology of the 580 series:

"We built a new machine, but we used the same technologies. We had the same basic chips, the same as we had on the 580. We were able to get the CPU cycle time significantly faster, fix a few things on the CPU, and do a lot of stuff in the storage area and the input-output (I/O) area. We tried to reuse some of the design, even to the point of not changing the I/O and console cycle time, so we actually had some interesting creative three-to-two cycle clocks for the input-output processors and the console. The console was redesigned fairly significantly because it had some reliability problems on the 580.... The 5890 was an excellent machine."[12]

Customers wanted to believe in the new systems, but they reacted with caution. Amdahl's sales force, which had only recently recovered from 580 shellshock, also wanted to believe in the 5890 models. To rekindle enthusiasm and confidence, Zemke, who had been with Amdahl only five months at this point, drew on his IBM experience, as he would recall in 1996:

"I brought in the whole sales force from all around the world to announce the 5890 in October 1985. Every group was teamed up with

A 5890 system with keyboard and operator. The system was similar to the 580 series, but with improvements in design and performance.

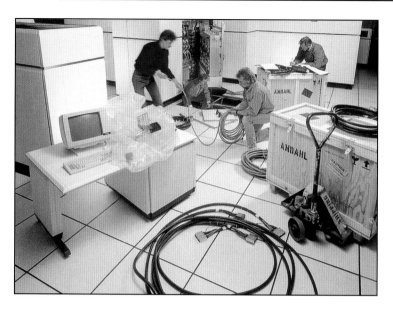

Above and right: A 5890 system is unpacked and tested by Amdahl engineers.

somebody from engineering or somebody from manufacturing. We broke them up in ten-person groups, and they were walked through the factory. The guys would say, 'There's a new machine, and boy, are we proud of it. We know the 580 was hard on you, but we got this one right, and it's going to be super.' By the end of that three-day meeting, the sales force was fired up and ready to go. They were confident."[13]

The 5890, like the mainframes before it, contained chips and subassemblies manufactured by Fujitsu. Zemke, however, was quick to point out, "This is our machine. We developed it. We built it. We own it."[14]

The Market Reacts

The first 5890 system was shipped in June 1986 to the Dallas-based Southland Corporation headquarters, where it was installed in less than 24 hours. The $12.8 billion corporation owned the 7-Eleven convenience store chain, the largest in the nation, and had been an Amdahl customer since 1977.[15] The fact that the 5890-300 supported IBM's MVS/XA operating system from the beginning contributed to its initial success.[16] Early 5890s would also be installed in university

computer centers in London and Manchester, replacing older 470V/8 models.[17]

In August 1986, Amdahl held two briefings to reassure reporters and analysts that the 5890 processor was off to a good start,[18] pointing out that performance levels of the 5890-300 were actually 10 percent higher than originally expected.[19]

But it wasn't until the final quarter of 1986 that Amdahl was able to reach volume production of the 5890-300 and began to generate serious returns on its investment. It was a testament to the power of the line that more than 40 Model 5890-300s were sold during the fourth quarter alone.

Amdahl's Other Businesses

Before the 5890 launch, Amdahl's share of the $12 billion annual mainframe market slipped to 8 percent, with National Advanced Systems holding a 2 percent share and IBM claiming the

remaining 90 percent.[20] But IBM's enormous market share did not intimidate Zemke. In fact, he saw it as an opportunity. "The stronger IBM gets, the better our opportunity," he told a reporter in 1985. "People are going to start looking at IBM's market share and question the wisdom of it. We are poised to take advantage of this."[21]

In February, IBM announced another price reduction on its 3090 and 308X series of mainframes, along with volume discount pricing.[22] CEO Jack Lewis was not intimidated either. Interviewed by a reporter at the time of the announcement, he reiterated Amdahl's basic strategy. "We try to sell on the basis of features and support rather than roll in the dirt on price."[23]

Later in the year, Anthony Pozos, Joseph Francesconi and Bruce Beebe were all promoted to senior vice president. Pozos would head human resources and corporate services, Francesconi would head the new marketing, service and communications products areas, and Beebe would continue leading mainframe and storage engineering and manufacturing operations.[24]

Intent on continuing its expansion across the industry, Amdahl introduced new products throughout 1985 and 1986.

The most successful of Amdahl's non-mainframe products were data storage units. A new 6680 Electronic Direct Access Storage (EDAS) product featured 256-kilobit chip technology that decreased access time to one-tenth that of IBM's 3380 storage device.[25] "By allowing users to migrate their performance-oriented data to a separate box, the solid-state EDAS frees up spinning media to do the things that they do best," said Don Feinstein, a storage products manager.[26]

Amdahl also added models AE4 and BE4 to its 6380 Storage System. These models doubled the storage capacity of standard 6380 models without increasing floor space and became one of 1986's most important product introductions. Priced at $78,510 for a Model BE4 and $104,110

for a Model AE4, both became available for general delivery in the fourth quarter of 1986.[27]

On the software front, Amdahl begin delivering the UTS/580 in mid-1986. UTS/580 software, designed for engineering and scientific multi-user applications, would be available as a stand-alone Unix operating system on 580 and 5890 processors or as a guest running under IBM's VM operating system.[28]

Amdahl had also been experimenting with an MVS/XA-type operating system called Aspen. A pet project of Bill O'Connell, Amdahl's senior vice president of strategic planning, Aspen's key feature was its ability to fine-tune itself, resulting in faster speeds with fewer programmers.

The system had been tried at 20 installations over the previous two years with modest success, but industry observers did not expect it to do well in a market saturated by IBM's dominant MVS operating system, in part because IBM users would not want to risk using an alternative since there were so many interfaces to match. "When you're talking about a plug-compatible operating system, you can't afford to make any mistakes," explained industry analyst Mike Chuba of the Gartner Group. "It will be very difficult to convince a user that he should forgo IBM and go with an alternative."[29]

True to the predictions of analysts, Amdahl scrapped Aspen in 1987.[30]

Amdahl Europe

In late 1984, Amdahl established a new European headquarters at the 800-year-old Dogmersfield Park estate in Hartley Wintney, England. The Georgian mansion, where, according

The 800-year-old Dogmersfield Park estate in England became the home for Amdahl's European headquarters in 1984.

to legend, Henry VIII met Katharine of Aragon, would house Amdahl International Management Services, Limited, the organization responsible for marketing and servicing customers in Europe and the Middle East.

After a two-year restoration of the building, which had been damaged by fire, the structure was featured in one of Prince Charles' books about architecture. Amdahl added 40,000 square feet of 18th century-style buildings to bring total office space to 90,000 square feet. Costs for additions and equipment ran in excess of $15 million. Amdahl President Jack Lewis and European General Manager Peter Williams were joined by Great Britain's Princess Anne during opening celebrations.

At the time, Amdahl employed about 1,000 people in Europe.[31] Alan Bell, recruited by Amdahl in 1977, was put in charge of European customer service. He would later take charge of all European operations, become senior vice president of worldwide field operations in 1998 and be named president of Amdahl's Global Solutions Group in 1999. Before joining Amdahl, he had been a large-systems engineer at IBM, working in the United Kingdom.[32]

As 1986 drew to a close, the company was in a good position to reflect upon its successes. Driven by the 5890, total revenue at $966.4 million was just shy of the $1 billion mark. Even better, net income increased 92 percent to top off at $68.9 million.[33] As a reflection of Amdahl's diversification, mainframe sales composed only 57 percent of total revenue, and the company was doing well in all of its business areas.[34]

Opening celebrations at Amdahl International Management Services, Limited, headquarters at Dogmersfield Park estate. Pictured are (standing) European headquarters General Manager Peter V. Williams, President and CEO Jack Lewis and (seated) Princess Anne.

Industry experts were predicting a slowdown in the demand for data processing systems in the immediate future, but Amdahl officers felt the scope of the company's product offerings would offset any ill effects.[35]

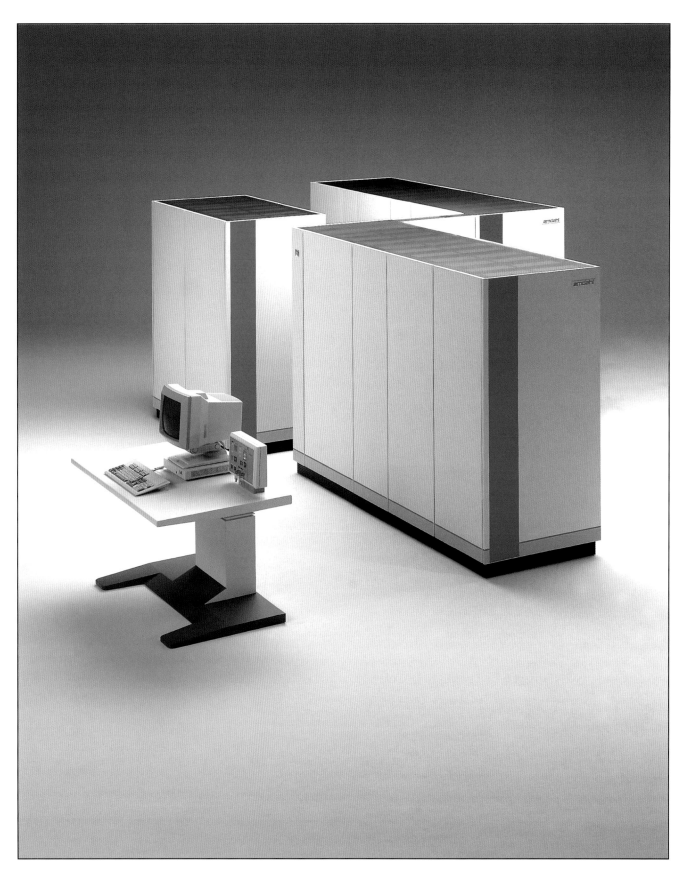

The introduction of the 5990 series in May 1988 was a milestone for both Amdahl and the mainframe industry.

CHAPTER EIGHT

HITTING THE MARK
1987–1989

"Amdahl's new-found respect owes much to Chairman Lewis' insight that offering products that are only cheaper and faster than IBM's is no longer enough. So Amdahl has begun offering features that IBM doesn't."

— Forbes, 1987[1]

CONTRARY TO MANY INDUSTRY predictions, the mainframe market did not collapse in the late 1980s. In fact, in many ways these last years of the decade were the golden age of Amdahl's mainframes and mainframe computing in general. No longer was a mainframe used as a single computing powerhouse; increasingly, companies were stringing terminals together and forming a company-wide network with the mainframe as a nucleus.

A Traditional Focus

Amdahl had a small customer base, consisting mostly of large corporations with sophisticated computing needs. "Whatever their problems are, we've got to solve them if we're going to be relevant to them. That drives our strategy and always will," said CEO Jack Lewis.[2]

Additional models of the successful 5890 series, including the 5890-400E three-way processor, the 5890-190E uniprocessor, and the 5890-180E entry-level uniprocessor, offered even more performance options and at least one important advantage over IBM's vaunted System 3090 models 300E and 400E — they could be upgraded simply by changing circuit boards.

Reliability Research, Inc., of Norwalk, Connecticut, rated the Model 5890-300 as one of the most reliable mainframes in operation, a distinction it shared with National Advanced Systems' Model AS/XL 60. Both systems averaged a mean time of six months between failures.[3]

"We are the premier designer of big IBM-compatible commercial computers," Lewis told *InformationWEEK* magazine. "It is the only thing we do: worry about how big users run data-processing shops. We spend 100 percent of our time on that. Anything we can do — in hardware, software, storage or communications — to help the user be more efficient, we'll do. That is the way we view the world."[4]

To take advantage of growing demand, Amdahl announced late in the first quarter that the company would boost its domestic sales staff by as much as 80 percent. The company also said it would spend 25 percent of its research and development budget on software.

Financial results for the first quarter of 1987 offered a taste of the success waiting for Amdahl Corporation in the months to come. Revenue rose 59 percent to $318.5 million, and income increased nearly 1,000 percent to $25.2 million.

The VLSI (very large system integration) logic chip used in the 5990 family of computers. The tower on top was used to dissipate heat.

International Situations

In April 1987, Amdahl became involved in an international trade dispute between Japan and the United States. The Reagan administration threatened to impose higher tariffs on Japanese chipmakers, accusing them of illegally dumping their chips on international markets and limiting sales of American chips to Japan. Amdahl, which depended on Fujitsu, Ltd., components for its various product lines, calculated that the tariff would cost the company an estimated $100 million annually. "The impact of the proposed tariff increase on our product categories ... is not a mere ricochet inflicting some economic pain," Jack Lewis argued. "It is a bullet coming straight at the heart of the company we have built over the last 17 years."[5] National Semiconductor joined Amdahl in successfully urging the Reagan administration not to impose tariffs.

As this debate raged, the company took action in another international arena when it sold its

In 1987, Amdahl began bonding wires with laser beams for better connections.

May 1987 — Jack Lewis becomes chairman of the board at Amdahl and Gene White becomes vice chairman.

May 1987 — Joe Zemke becomes president.

September 1987 — The 4725 series of front-end communications processors is introduced.

subsidiary, Amdahl South Africa, amid growing international condemnation of that country's system of apartheid. In doing so, Amdahl joined hundreds of companies and governments that pressured the white minority rulers of that troubled nation to ease its racist policies.

A Change in Leadership

At Amdahl's board meeting in May, directors named Lewis, who was already CEO, chairman of the board. Gene White was named vice chairman, and Joe Zemke added the responsibilities of president to his duties as chief operating officer. All three men would continue to bring their particular focus to company operations. Lewis remained in charge of long-term strategy, White specialized in strategic external developments, and Zemke oversaw internal, daily activities.[6]

Amdahl's new UTS/580 Release 1.2 brought additional enhancements to the company's Unix-based mainframe operating system.[7] Such enhancements were becoming increasingly important as the role of the mainframe evolved beyond the data center to systems serving Unix workstations within even larger distributed networks.

The Communications Market

Amdahl's commitment to research and development remained constant. In 1987, the company devoted more than $179 million to research and development, up from $135 million in 1986. Some of its efforts went toward developing a new generation of communication processors that would connect data processing centers with thousands of users.

Introduced in September 1987, the 4725 series consisted of models 4725-30 and 4725-40.[8] These processors, developed in conjunction with Fujitsu, employed emitter-coupled logic (ECL) and proprietary 20,000-gate CMOS (complementary metal-oxide semiconductor) technology, providing a 30-nanosecond cycle time.

Bell Canada was one of the first customers to use the Model 4725-40. The phone company's Montreal office contained one of two data processing centers that supported 15,000 users. As Bill Caroli, communications product manager for Amdahl's Peripheral Products Division, pointed out, "Unlike some other vendors, who require you to license software from them, we just drop our communications processors into a customer set-

1987 — Amdahl crosses the billion-dollar mark in annual sales.

February 1989 — Amdahl acquires Key Computer Laboratories of Fremont, California.

May 1988 — The next generation of mainframes, the 5990 series, is introduced.

April 1989 — Amdahl expands the 5990 series with three additional processors.

ting. They don't have to change any software. Amdahl's commitment to compatibility and performance gave our communications processors a longer useful life than our competitors' offerings."[9]

In May 1988, the division introduced the 4745 series communication processors, which offered 40 percent more throughput than IBM's most advanced communications controllers and sold within a $90,000 to $120,000 price range. The processors could also be connected to AMDAC for on-line support. Certification of 4725 and 4745 compatibility with new generations of software continued into the late 1990s with more than 90 percent of total production still installed and supported by the company at the end of 1997.[10]

While Amdahl kept its communications processors, its Communications Systems Division,

an outgrowth of Amdahl's 1980 Tran Telecommunications acquisition, had failed to meet revenue goals. "The lost opportunity pales when compared to the expense," explained Jack Lewis in 1996. "It was the opportunity to participate in a major marketplace in a significant way, but we weren't able to figure out how to make it happen. In some respects, we were probably too early, and that combined with our probably poor execution."[11]

In August 1989, Amdahl consolidated what remained of its communications systems pro-

Amdahl's Communications Systems Division offered products such as these MTS Multiplexers, which improved network communications for customers. Parts of the division were sold in 1988.

duction to create the Amdahl Communications Products Group. The new communications group would be directed by Samuel H. Ezekiel, formerly general manager of Amdahl's Communications Systems Division in Richardson, Texas. For a period, the group would continue producing network products previously made by the defunct division.[12]

A Billion-Dollar Company

Amdahl revenues easily achieved the coveted $1 billion mark for the first time in 1987, reaching $1.5 billion and producing net income of $146 million, a 249 percent increase over 1986.[13] The company also had doubled its number of *Fortune* 500 customer accounts since 1985, from 12 to 26 accounts.[14] A staggering 85 percent of sales were attributed to the 5890 series, making it the most successful product in Amdahl history.[15] Amdahl had a five-year growth rate averaging 17 percent annually and was ranked fifth in profit and sixth in sales among Silicon Valley's top 100 firms.[16]

The drive toward workplace connectivity continued in 1988, when Amdahl announced a product development and marketing agreement with Sun Microsystems, Inc. The two companies would integrate Sun Microsystems' operating software for workstations (SunOS) with Amdahl's UTS operating software, creating a Unix-based system by which workstation users could access Amdahl processors.

Sun Microsystems President Scott McNeally saw the integration as being "particularly important to scientists and engineers who depend on workstations for specialized operations and who need the performance and memory of a mainframe."[17] By this time, Unix products and marketing accounted for 15 percent of Amdahl's business.[18]

Though this initial agreement with Sun had only a minor impact on business in the 1980s, it created a solid foundation for a pact in late 1993 under which Amdahl became a value-added reseller of Sun servers, a business that eventually would generate more than $150 million in revenues annually for Amdahl.

The 5990 Series Breakthrough

In May 1988, Amdahl proudly launched its next generation of mainframe computers, the 5990 series. This series changed the entire mainframe industry in several ways. For one thing, its introduction marked only the second time a plug-compatible mainframe manufacturer had introduced the next evolutionary advance in processor performance ahead of IBM.[19] It would be another two months before IBM introduced its comparable 3090-S series.[20] Secondly, the 5990-1400 was the first processor with a total computing capacity above 100 MIPS (millions of instructions per second). *The Wall Street Journal* praised the 5990 as "a milestone — both for the industry and for Amdahl."[21]

Processors in the 5990 series, including the 5990-700 dual processor and the 5990-1400 four-way multiprocessor, featured dense ECL circuitry that enabled the system's entire central processing unit to be contained within a single, multi-layer circuit board. As a result, the system was nearly twice as powerful as previous processors, with a remarkable 10-nanosecond cycle time. Priced at $7 million, the 5990-700 would be available in June 1988. The larger 5990-1400, priced at

Quality management teams such as this one helped Amdahl cross the billion-dollar sales mark in 1987.

$13 million, would hit the market by the end of the year.[22]

The 5990 series had been developed by Fujitsu and modified by Amdahl. It incorporated the same chip and board technology as Fujitsu's non-IBM-compatible M-780, but Amdahl was responsible for overall 5990 design and assembly of the components into finished processor systems at its manufacturing facilities in Ireland and California. It took the companies more than three years and $300 million to bring the series to market.[23] This joint project involved a team of Amdahl engineers working closely with a team of Fujitsu engineers.[24]

To announce the series, the company assembled 28 teams to introduce the new mainframes to customers in 130 cities around the world in what would become "the most successful product launch in company history."[25]

Within the next year, Amdahl also expanded its data storage product line with the 6100 storage processor and the 6380J and 6380K disk storage drives. The 6100, the most advanced stor-age processor on the market, offered four times the throughput and twice the capacity and connectivity to host mainframes as competitive products.[26]

Amdahl further expanded its storage product line in June 1989 with the introduction of the solid-state 6110 high-performance storage subsystem.[27]

Strong Management

Amdahl could close the books on 1988 with a great deal of satisfaction. Revenues for the year reached $1.8 billion, yielding net income of $223 million.[28] Perhaps more importantly, Amdahl's share of the $8.2 billion mainframe market increased from 13 percent to 16 percent during the year.[29]

Commenting on Amdahl's executive management, a Wall Street investment advisor noted, "I

Amdahl employees celebrated the first shipment of a 5990 computer in 1988.

The conductive cooling module used in the 5990 series.

think they have a very strong grasp of exactly how the mainframe market is evolving, and the steps they have taken have put them exactly in concert with this evolution of the environment. They have made a very clever strategic alliance with Fujitsu. This management is just a standout."[30]

Early in 1989, Amdahl acquired Key Computer Laboratories, a 60-person firm based in Fremont, California. Founded in 1987 by former members of Valid Logic Systems, Key Computer Laboratories specialized in Unix systems and high-performance scientific computer technologies. According to Lewis, the acquisition would provide "fresh insight into new design techniques that may interest us in the future." The acquisition cost Amdahl about $30 million in stock.[31]

Expanding the 5990 Series

In April, Amdahl added three new processors to its successful 5990 series: The 5990-350 uniprocessor for modest entry-level computing requirements, the 5990-500 entry-level dual processor, and the 5990-1100 three-way multiprocessor. All three models also featured an enhanced Multiple Domain Feature that increased the number of domains from four to seven in dual and uniprocessors and from eight to 14 in multiprocessors operating in partitioned mode. Together, these new systems offered customers a wide range of options and upgrade paths.[32]

The rapid financial and product growth at Amdahl during the previous two years created additional demand for new facilities. In Santa Clara County alone, the company already occupied 26 buildings with a total of 1.7 million square feet. Yet this was not enough. Amdahl added another 290,000 square feet with the purchase of four buildings in northern San Jose. The purchase included an empty five-acre lot, and in July, the company added another 13.38 acres of undeveloped land to the tract. Amdahl did not occupy all of the buildings immediately but planned to move to the new facilities gradually as the need arose.[33]

A World Record and a Helping Hand

In August 1989, six Amdahl researchers made history when they discovered the largest prime number to date. A prime number is a whole number not evenly divisible by any number other than the numeral one and itself. Scientists often test the speed and power of computers by having them search for new, increasingly large prime numbers, a process that requires millions of computations since each number must be tested by dividing it by every number before it. The new prime number discovered by Amdahl scientists contained 65,087 digits. It beat the world record, set by Cray Research, Inc., in 1985, by 37 digits.[34]

On October 17, 1989, northern California was rocked by a rush-hour earthquake measuring 6.9 on the Richter Scale, making it one of the strongest in an area known for earthquakes. Candlestick Park, packed with a World Series crowd, trembled, while highways crumbled and bridges collapsed, including parts of the Bay Bridge, used by hundreds of thousands of commuters daily. Silicon Valley, however, escaped the worst of the damage.

Amdahl responded to the emergency by helping its less fortunate neighbors nearby, where power companies needed emergency back-up communication systems. The company shipped systems from its communications production facility in Ontario, Canada, to the San Francisco Bay Area, where they were immediately installed, easing pressure on the region's communication networks. Pacific Bell telephone staff analyst Terry LaRue praised the company's efforts: "Within 48 hours of placing the order, we had equipment on site. Amdahl really came through!"[35]

The 5990 series was expanded to include several new models that were popular with customers.

Amdahl's Sunnyvale headquarters in 1989.

Price Wars

As the decade drew to a close, Amdahl realized its successes did not come without a price. IBM responded to the successful 5990 line with an aggressive price war that took its toll. Even though Amdahl was selling more systems than ever, its net income was dropping. In the third quarter of 1989, for example, revenue increased 15 percent but net income dropped 37 percent. Bob Djurdjevic, president of Annex Research, observed, "The company is adding sales people. Revenues and shipments are up; in fact, they are higher than expected. But there have been margin pressures, and that calls for cost reductions."[36]

Late in 1989, Amdahl laid off 5 percent of its workforce, reducing total employees to 8,300 worldwide. "This is a difficult and unpleasant situation, but we're trying to make it as painless as possible," said Tony Pozos, senior vice president for human resources.[37]

Amdahl closed the year with a phenomenal posting of $2.1 billion in revenue, although the price wars forced net income down 30 percent to $153 million.[38]

To foster communication with employees, the company established the Amdahl Television Network in 1990.

CHAPTER NINE

A TIME OF TRANSITION
1990–1992

"We will remember 1991 as a time when we learned to deal with uncertainty and to manage for business conditions we had not planned."

— President Joe Zemke[1]

IN FEBRUARY 1990, RUMORS began circulating through the industry of a possible takeover of Amdahl by Fujitsu, Limited. The speculation was fueled by a clause in the 1984 agreement that limited Fujitsu's ownership to 49.5 percent. The agreement would not expire until 1994, but either company could cancel it during the second quarter of 1990. Wall Street analysts, noting Hitachi Data Systems' purchase of National Semiconductor's mainframe operation a year earlier, raised the possibility of a Fujitsu buyout.

The analysts overlooked some important factors, however. If Amdahl was acquired by Fujitsu, there was a good chance that the loyalty and team spirit of Amdahl's engineering and manufacturing organizations could be damaged unless there was widespread support for the merger, which there was not in the spring of 1990. Unlike Amdahl, National Semiconductor's mainframe business lacked engineering and manufacturing elements, functioning solely as a marketing unit for Hitachi's mainframe computers. It did not have to rely on the engineers that were so valuable to Amdahl.[2]

Amdahl and Fujitsu had a mutually beneficial relationship. With Amdahl already bringing in more than $2 billion in annual revenue, what could Fujitsu gain with a major reorganiza-

tion? Fujitsu executives squelched the buyout rumors.[3]

In 1990, Amdahl began a serious effort to strengthen its market position through a reorganization to focus on several different markets. In May, Amdahl consolidated its Unix operations under the leadership of Joseph J. Francesconi (an Amdahl veteran who would later leave the company to become president and CEO of Network Equipment Technologies, a robust $350 million communications business). Reporting to Francesconi would be Bill Ferone, vice president of Unix systems; Eric L. Miles, vice president of systems software; Mike Taylor, vice president of systems architecture; and David L. Anderson, vice president of advanced systems.[4] President Joe Zemke discussed the logic behind the management realignment in *Electronic News*:

"While the same sales force sells both Unix and IBM-compatible systems, the product development, the marketing, the strategy, the pricing — all of those things — need two different mechanisms. One is aimed at a market that is pretty pre-

In 1989, the National Black Association recognized Amdahl as a valuable corporate partner.

dictable, where the prices are set by IBM, and the architectures are also set by IBM. In that market, we're really responding and, in some cases, trying to stay ahead of them in features and functions.... Unix is a market that's wide open. There are lots of players. It's not very well defined. It's still emerging ... and so it is much more demanding in terms of seeing over the horizon."[5]

The reorganization of Amdahl's Unix operations was partially prompted by disappointing sales of UTS software and the Model 7300 processor,[6] which was targeted to fill the gap between Unix minicomputers and more powerful 5890 and 5990 mainframes.[7] As then–vice president of Unix Systems Bill Ferone explained, "What we are experiencing so far is that the 7300 is receiving a tremendous amount of interest, but a 7300 transaction turns into a 5990 or a 5890 sale." Amdahl would later combine the marketing of its Unix sys-

During Management Awareness Day in 1990, senior executives worked a variety of jobs. Here Vice President for manufacturing William Flanagan (background) adjusts a computer cable.

September 1990 — Amdahl announces the powerful 5995 series of mainframes.

September 1990 — UTS 2.1, an enhanced version of the Unix operating system, is introduced.

March 1991 — The Huron applications development and production system is introduced.

tems software with its Unix hardware projects, although the 7300 system would never become a viable product.[8]

The 5995M Series

In September 1990, Amdahl announced its next generation of mainframe computers, the 5995 series, which would be the most powerful line of computers in the IBM-compatible marketplace. The series consisted of six 5995A models based on the same design as the earlier 5990 sys-

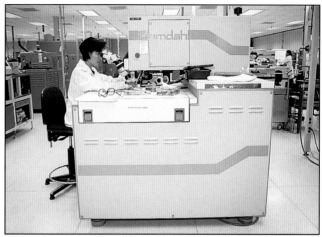

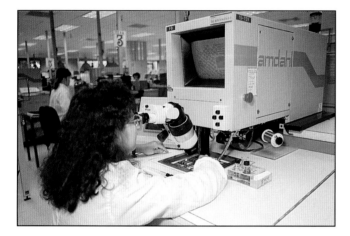

Above and left: The manufacturing at Amdahl required tremendous attention to detail.

tems for large-scale data processing applications, and four revolutionary new 5995M models designed for even more demanding requirements.

A single 5995M processor had operating speeds as high as 54 MIPS (millions of instructions per second). This made them the most powerful processors on the market, surpassing systems

May 1991 — Enhancements to the Model 4745 Communications Processor are announced.

May 1992 — Joe Zemke promoted to chief executive officer.

September 1991 — Amdahl voted the top-quality supplier in a Key Associates/*Computer Weekly* survey.

July 1992 — New versions of Amdahl's Huron system extend its usefulness to smaller platforms and open systems.

made by Fujitsu (50 MIPS, though unavailable in the United States), Hitachi Data Systems (45 MIPS) and IBM (41 MIPS). The top-of-the-line 5995-8650M with eight of the processors maxed out at 323 MIPS — a full 123 MIPS more computing capacity than IBM's ES/9000 six-way multiprocessor.[9]

Developing the 5995M series had taken five years, 800 engineers and $500 million. Another $200 million was spent on facilities and equipment to manufacture and test the new generation.[10] The first models were shipped in December 1991.[11]

Closing the books on 1990, Amdahl saw a 3 percent rise in revenue to $2.2 billion for the year, with a net income of $184 million. Amdahl's customer base had grown 15 percent in each of the previous two years. For the third year in a row, the company ranked first in overall customer satisfaction in Datapro Research Corporation's annual survey of mainframe users.[12]

Open Systems

Over the previous years, customers had expressed a growing interest in open systems such as Unix, which did not rely on a single supplier's proprietary architecture. Open systems instead operate on widely accepted industry standards. This allows hardware and software from several vendors to work together within a single computing complex. Amdahl met this interest with a long-range strategy that would allow customers to use open architecture and proprietary systems side-by-side. The company chose Sun Microsystems, Inc.'s Scalable Processor Architecture (SPARC) chip on which to standardize its Unix development work on open systems products. The SPARC chip was made popular by Sun Microsystems' workstations, and Fujitsu was one of the SPARC chip's suppliers.[13]

Amdahl employees celebrate the sale of the first 5995M in 1991.

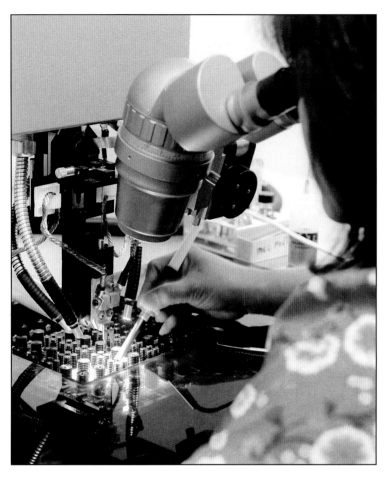

Above and right: Technicians working in Amdahl manufacturing facilities in the early 1990s.

nized data from Unix and X.25 networks for application to a UTS-based mainframe system. "The main point here is that the more homogeneous your network is from the start, the easier it will be to manage," observed Robert Kidd, an analyst at Dataquest in San Jose.[16]

The Unix market greeted Amdahl's UTS 2.1 operating system warmly. The UTS system was widely used in the telecommunications industry, and the federal government chose UTS 2.1 to support the Government Open Systems Interconnection Protocol (GOSIP) over IBM's mainframe Unix offering.[17]

The Huron System

In March 1991, Amdahl introduced the Huron system after ten years of development. The soft-

In September 1990, Amdahl improved its Unix-based offerings with the introduction of the UTS 2.1 operating system, advanced Unix software for proprietary System 390 mainframes that enabled customers to link workstations, minicomputers and supercomputers to a central processor.[14] UTS 2.1 also extended its ability to work in IBM virtual machine (VM) and multiple virtual storage (MVS) operating environments, where it could be installed side-by-side with those other operating systems without interrupting existing applications. It was hoped that UTS 2.1 would increase Amdahl's annual Unix software and related hardware businesses.[15]

Also improving Amdahl's offerings to Unix customers were the new Model 4655 front-end communication processors. These systems orga-

Chairman and CEO Jack Lewis and Vice Chairman Gene White stand with Amdahl veterans at a 20th anniversary award dinner.

ware was designed to reduce the amount of time required to develop new applications software by acting like a translator between the application codes of different operating systems. It could be used on a wide variety of computers, from large-scale to personal work stations.[18] In addition, it opened the door to an entirely new line of business for Amdahl.

Huron had been developed by Helge Knudsen, a brilliant Danish scientist who had joined Amdahl in 1977. He formulated the idea during his first three years with the company, while he was helping set up subsidiaries throughout northern Europe.

In 1981, Senior Vice President Bill O'Connell persuaded him to establish a small research and development center in Canada. A group of young, dedicated scientists — usually fewer than eight people — toiled for several years in a tiny, windowless office. At first, few people at Amdahl even knew they existed.

Throughout the long development process, Knudsen never wavered from the ambitious objectives he had formulated in Europe. As he recounted years later:

"The first objective was to build adaptable, maintainable, extendible applications. The next objective was to reuse program and data elements. The com-

puter industry at the time was the only industry where you built everything from scratch instead of using reusable models. The third objective was to provide transparent access to existing data. In other words, to provide integration with old systems. The fourth objective spanned across all the others. It was to have general-purpose production performance. Namely, even if we have all these adaptable, maintainable, extendible and reusable components and access to existing systems, we would still have standard performance.... In the computer industry, everybody wants more functionality, more graphics, more this and more that. But if it doesn't meet the standard acceptable performance, nobody wants it after all. So, these were the four objectives that I have had for 20 years. Actually, we did awfully well on that."[19]

The first Huron system went online May 1, 1986. It was simply a prototype, set up to see how it would work. With the success of this prototype and others that followed, the Huron project finally got a formal business plan. In 1987, after the air conditioning broke in their small office, the engineers moved to a larger one. By 1991, more than 20 prototypes had been set up with such prestigious clients as the Bank of Montreal and American Express Travel Related Industries. The small staff had expanded to include a viable support organization. It was time to formally introduce the product to the market.

Instead of keeping Huron as a small entrepreneurial project, the executives decided to incorporate the product throughout the company. Zemke and Lewis saw the Huron system as an opportunity to reduce the company's reliance on hardware development and sales.

The transition presented some challenges for Amdahl. The sales force was used to comparing its compatible mainframes with IBM mainframes. Explaining and selling an entirely new product, one without a strong competing product to compare it with, was a new experience.

"We have just laid Amdahl's credibility on the line with this product," said O'Connell. "We are not trying to be a software supplier. We are trying to solve problems."[20]

The Huron application development software proved extremely popular with some customers but did not have the market impact Amdahl hoped for. The British government's version of the IRS, called Inland Revenue, claimed that the Huron system was four times more productive than standard application development tools.

Huron compared more than favorably to AD/ Cycle, its IBM competitor, which was subsequently abandoned. The biggest problem for customers using AD/Cycle was that by the time an application was developed, the user's needs had changed. Adjustments at this stage were difficult and expensive. Huron, on the other hand, was easy to change. Another benefit of Huron was that it took only three days to teach users the fundamentals of the system.[21]

Knudsen left Amdahl in 1994 and became president and CEO of Great Lakes Research and Development, a Toronto company he established with Amdahl support.[22]

New Products

Early In 1991, Amdahl introduced an enhancement to the Model 4745 Communications Processor. By incorporating Static Random Access Memory (SRAM) chip technology, the cycle time needed to access memory was significantly reduced, and the Model 4745's channel connectivity capability was increased from six channels to eight channels. Units would be available by the third quarter.[23]

Amdahl's financial situation, however, had been declining since the beginning of the year. In the second quarter, revenue dropped 13 percent to $450 million while net income plunged 86 percent, to $6.3 million. Meanwhile, IBM's profits dropped 92 percent. Both companies attributed the shortfalls to the sluggish European economy.[24] However, Amdahl's situation was worse since the company relied so heavily on mainframes, said Henry Cassel, an Amdahl marketing executive. "We still depended very much on the mainframe. Growth used to be 30 percent and prices dropped 15 percent per year. Then those things reversed and growth was 15 percent and prices dropped 30 percent. It doesn't take a spreadsheet genius to figure out that that dog won't hunt."[25] Heavy costs associated with new product development were also hurting the bottom line.

Adding to Amdahl's problems were difficulties in its storage products organization. Shipments of the next generation Model 6390 Direct Access Storage Device (DASD) had fallen behind sched-

Amdahl employees constantly found ways to upgrade their skills. Here is a class that graduated from business studies at DeAnza College.

ule. The delay was attributed to microcode problems associated with Amdahl's proprietary controller, the 6100 Storage Processor. To make matters worse, IBM was ready to ship its next generation of DASD, the 3390 Model 3, and Hitachi Data Systems had already delivered its new generation, with plans to begin volume shipments of advanced models by the middle of 1992.[26]

Throughout the year, Amdahl would continue to be plagued with problems in the storage products division. Model 6380K DASDs manufactured between June and September had a defect that could lead to loss of data. Even though few customers experienced such a difficulty, Amdahl informed everyone who had purchased the systems, and the company provided replacements for the faulty disk enclosure units.[27]

By late November, the new Model 6390 DASD was ready for shipment.

The marketplace for the company's UTS system was also beginning to see growth as the traditional Unix market expanded beyond scientific and telecommunications applications to financial

Topnotch employees were critical to the success of Amdahl. College recruiting booths such as this helped the company find new talent.

institutions, banks, and even the automobile industry, where UTS functioned as a file server for work stations.[28]

In addition, customer confidence in Amdahl remained high. In September, Amdahl was voted the top-quality supplier in a Key Associates/ *Computer Weekly* survey of more than 2,000 large system users. The company was rated far ahead of the competition with its competitively priced products and services. The company's products, sales force, staff capabilities and senior management were singled out for particular praise.[29]

In the mainframe arena, the 5995M models were in their final stage of debugging, with limited deliveries of the three-way and four-way multiprocessor models set for late 1991 and volume shipments scheduled for April of 1992. Analysts expected company revenue to climb, and some of them upgraded Amdahl's stock from sell to buy.[30]

Prices for the 5995M series, however, were reduced as much as 11 percent in response to IBM's new product announcements,[31] and financial results continued to reflect a downward trend. Revenue for the third quarter of 1991 fell to $419.3 million, with net income resting at $5.5 million.[32] Though sales remained slow in Europe, they were steady throughout the United States, Canada and the Pacific Rim.[33]

The situation was not destined to improve as the year drew to a close. During the fourth quarter of 1991, revenue dropped nearly 40 percent to $390 million, resulting in a loss of $2.7 million — the first operating loss since the company went public in 1976. The disk drive problems and weak European market were partly to blame, as were the costs of developing new products and delayed purchases by customers waiting until the next generation of systems became available.

Total revenue for 1991 was $1.7 billion, down from $2.2 billion the year before, and net income plunged 98 percent to $4.4 million. "It will be a great year to make comparisons against," was the wry comment of CFO Edward F. Thompson.[34] President Zemke described the year as a learning experience.

"We will remember 1991 as a time when we learned to deal with uncertainty and to manage for business conditions we had not planned."[35]

In early 1992, Amdahl introduced an enhancement to its 6390 DASD, a module that expanded capacity by 50 percent within the same footprint. Customers also had the option of populating their frames with four, eight, 12 or 16 channels.[36]

In late 1991 and early 1992, Fujitsu, Limited, purchased additional Amdahl shares, raising its holdings to 44.76 percent of the stock. When Amdahl employees bought shares through stock purchase and stock option plans, Fujitsu's ownership percentage would slip, so the Japanese would occasionally buy blocks of shares to compensate for that dilution.[37]

Amdahl's financial picture wasn't improving, however, and to make matters worse, technical glitches began to surface. In early 1992, Amdahl found that it had to make repairs on production models of its 5995M mainframes, delaying shipments by several months. Problems with the computer's automated console system and software were cited as reasons for the delay.

However, the system had some reliability issues that would be expensive to fix, Zemke said:

"It was the 580 all over again, and it just about sunk us.... We had two problems. We had some design problems on our part. We had some technology problems from Fujitsu. Both of those would be fixed, but it was one of those moments of real truth. I knew the Amdahl people, and I knew our commitment. We would retroactively fix every machine that we put out there."[38]

Heavy demand for 5995M models since the initial December shipment caused a six-month backlog, which further added to scheduling conflicts. Analysts predicted that delays would create discounts for customers who waited, which would drive down profits despite the backlog.

In May 1992, Zemke was promoted to CEO. Jack Lewis remained chairman of the board. Lewis noted that the promotion "is consistent with our management succession plan for expanding the responsibilities of senior executives as the company grows and diversifies."[39] Gene White also remained as vice chairman, a position he would hold until his departure in mid-1993 to become chairman of a new Amdahl joint venture.[40]

Record Revenues and Falling Profits

As the third quarter of 1992 drew to a close, Amdahl's financial managers grew anxious as they tracked a disturbing trend. The company posted record revenues of $745 million but saw profits of only 2 cents a share.[41] The company had no alternative but to cut costs, said Ernest B. Thompson, vice president and controller:

"What it really says to you is the cost structure of the product is too high and probably prices are coming down faster than you thought they would. Talk about a wake-up call. It would not be the first time in the company's history that we had a reduction in force, but it was going to be big."[42]

Amdahl laid off 900 people, or 9 percent of its worldwide workforce of 9,700. Six hundred people were laid off in Sunnyvale and Santa Clara. Though of little consolation to fired workers, Amdahl wasn't the only company going through tough times. The layoffs, the largest in Amdahl history, marked the fifth significant layoff in Silicon Valley in a single month.[43] Amdahl took a pretax charge of $15 million to $20 million to pay for severance payments and layoff expenses, creating a net loss of $31 million for the quarter.[44]

As 1992 drew to a close, Amdahl's financial results continued their troubling pattern. Although revenue topped $2.5 billion, the highest ever, the company suffered a net loss of $7 million. Drastic change was needed if the company was going to reverse that trend.

Springboarding off Huron, Amdahl continued to expand its open systems offerings in the nineties.

CHAPTER TEN

Synergies
1993–1995

"If we're a customer-centric company, we should be looking at opportunities for our customers to use technology."
— Linda Alepin, 1996[1]

BY 1993, INDUSTRY SOOTH-sayers were loudly announcing the death of the mainframe. Personal computers and laptops had become the darlings of the computer industry, and sales of these products were booming while the mainframe market was becoming dangerously competitive — which was part of the reason Amdahl's profits fell even as revenue rose.

Concern about the mainframe had been building since the personal computer first made its appearance in the early 1980s. Businesses soon recognized personal computers as "smart" terminals that could perform some of the mainframe's traditional functions. Organizations began to build information networks with a combination of mainframes and personal computers. Amdahl went into 1993 looking for a way to fit itself into the new computing environment. According to President Jack Lewis:

"What happened was the terminals got very smart and there was a logical redistribution of the workload across the system. So obviously we weren't in the mainframe business, we were in the server business. It just happened that the environment was called a mainframe environment, but these systems can be servers too."[2]

It was a difficult time. The company's stock was at a 6½-year low, and the fact that other mainframe manufacturers were going through a similar slump was small comfort. Linda Alepin, an Amdahl employee since 1978 and vice president of marketing development until 1993, recalled working overtime, including pulling all-nighters, to put together a plan for Amdahl's future.

"I really couldn't have predicted exactly what was going to happen, but what I felt was that we really were not changing fast enough to meet the market. What the market was doing was going faster than we were."[3]

Amdahl was forced to further reduce its workforce to 7,400 people worldwide, with 4,350 employees in Silicon Valley.[4]

It was time for drastic change lest the downward spiral consume Amdahl. "It became clear that there was a fundamental shift in the marketplace, and we really had to look at our position and make a technology shift," said Treasurer Mike

Amdahl offered software solutions that allowed customers to maximize their investments in technology.

Shahbazian. "It was kind of like being on a burning bridge. We could go forward or backward. We decided to go forward."[5]

That translated into changing the company's basic approach to computing. In its very embryonic stages, Amdahl's plan was to increasingly market its mainframes as servers and provide complete server hardware, solutions and software. It was a landmark decision for Amdahl, which had built its reputation on more traditional applications within the mainframe marketplace. Nearly every employee had a mainframe background, yet, to survive, the company was pushing into new territory.

Antares Alliance Group

One of the first major steps came in June 1993, when the company and Electronic Data Systems Corporation (EDS), then a unit of General Motors Corporation, formed the Antares Alliance Group with Gene White as chairman and John Cavalier as its first president and CEO. Cavalier had been president and CEO for four leading-edge technology companies, vice president and general manager of two divisions of Apple Computer, and president of the computer division of Atari.

The motto "A Customer Problem Is an Amdahl Problem" graces the wall of the company's customer service headquarters.

June 1993 — Amdahl and Electronic Data Systems form the Antares Alliance Group.

September 1993 — Amdahl agrees to jointly develop Unix software and to sell Sun Microsystems' midrange SPARC server lines.

December 1993 — Amdahl gives Fujitsu responsibility for future mainframe development, design and manufacture.

The goal of the Dallas-based alliance was to use Huron as the base to provide development tools for business-related application software. The resulting software had to be flexible enough to be used across an entire computing enterprise. "You would use the product in mission-critical situations where you need to get up and running fast. Customers' businesses are changing rapidly, and they need to write applications quickly," said Cavalier.[6]

Amdahl, with 80 percent ownership, contributed its Huron applications development system to Antares, while EDS provided its InCASE data modeling and application-building system and COBOL conversion tools. In order to succeed, the system would have to work across several different hardware platforms, as Cavalier noted:

"We brought the architecture to the desktop and followed Microsoft standards. The result is a classic three-tiered architecture for software products that spans three hardware platforms. It works on a mainframe, works in the Unix world, and works in the Windows NT world."[7]

The name of the system was later changed from Huron to ObjectStar, to reflect that the technology was object oriented. "ObjectStar has the capability to seamlessly integrate and run blended solutions. No other product in the world can do that," Cavalier noted.

Reorganization

In August 1993, Amdahl announced a major reorganization of operations, creating five groups: Compatible Systems; Enterprise Storage Systems; the Antares Alliance Group; Customer Services, which accounted for a huge portion of Amdahl's revenues; and Open Enterprise Systems.

Research and development, marketing, and manufacturing were decentralized and placed under their respective groups, operating independently but reporting directly to the newly created Office of Field Operations, managed by Amdahl veterans David Wright, who headed the daily activities of the organization, and Ollie Nutt, who also served as chief of corporate marketing.[8]

The organization was designed to provide greater focus on software and open systems products that, combined with Amdahl's traditional IBM-compatible systems, would allow the company to offer a single solution for most customer require-

1994 — The Business Solutions Group (BSG) is formed.

1995 — Amdahl celebrates the 20th anniversary of the first mainframe shipment.

1994 — Amdahl forms the Business Solutions Group as part of the existing service organization.

1995 — Amdahl introduces the LVS storage system, nicknamed "Elvis."

Above: John Cavalier leading software developers and end users in a discussion of some of the solutions provided by Huron.

Below: Former pro football guard David Wright joined Amdahl in 1986, played key roles in the company's strategic reorganization and later became president and chief executive officer.

of desktop computing. In other words, enterprise-wide computing."[9]

In September 1993, Amdahl entered into another agreement to expand its open systems sales and expertise. This agreement called for Amdahl to sell Sun Microsystems' SPARCcenter servers, which formed multiprocessing configurations by linking workstations with personal computers and storage units. Scott McNeally, CEO for Sun Microsystems, commented that Amdahl's sales force was better equipped to sell the products, which cost as much as $1.7 million. "Sun's sales force isn't necessarily geared to this price point, but it's a tiny machine for Amdahl," he said.[10]

Within a week of the announcement, Amdahl's stock rose 18 percent, prompting analysts such as Bob Djurdjevic of Annex Research in Phoenix to observe, "Strategically, Amdahl is definitely taking a step in the right direction."[11]

David Wright, then executive vice president of the Enterprise Computing Group, said the relationship with Sun had the important side effect of boosting confidence within the corridors of Amdahl. "One of the things we learned from the Sun relationship was that not only did we need Sun, but Sun really needed us."[12]

Wright had an unusual background for a corporate executive. Before joining IBM, he had been an offensive guard for both the Chicago Bears and the New England Patriots in the early seventies. At age 27, he realized that professional football had stopped being fun and turned to a career in business:

ments. The benefits of this strategy were explained in company literature:

"As departmental operations expand, redundant resources and duplicated data undermine business operations. And the lack of communication between departments and the corporate data center impairs productivity, limiting the ability of the enterprise to compete. What's needed is a seamless integration of the two environments that provides the benefits of centralized management while preserving the advantages*

"I never had a summer off since I was in grade school. In college, at Xavier, I didn't know what spring break was. One day, I was walking into the Patriots camp, which at that time was in Amherst. I thought to myself, 'I don't think I'm having fun anymore. I'm going to have to make a decision.'"[13]

Wright, who had a degree in physics, was interviewed and hired by IBM. He worked for 12 years in sales, steadily rising through the ranks. In 1986, Wright accepted an offer at Amdahl as vice president of sales in the Eastern United States.

Amdahl Is the Architect

As with many companies caught in a transitional period, Amdahl continued to struggle. With roughly 2,000 customers worldwide and a workforce that had been further trimmed to 5,600, the company needed to carefully choose how it would allocate scarce resources between the new alliances and its traditional strengths.

This issue was important because Amdahl was at a critical point in the development of a powerful new mainframe: the Millennium. The proposed system used low-cost CMOS (complementary metal-oxide semiconductor) chips in place of ECL (emitter-coupled logic) technology.[14] With CMOS technology, more transistors and circuits could be packed onto a chip. CMOS chips were also much cheaper and more reliable than ECL technology. For example, the 5995M required 3,000 ECL chips, while the Millennium would require only 300 CMOS chips. Most importantly, Fujitsu already had experience with CMOS technology. Joe Zemke felt switching to CMOS was a good decision "for all kinds of reasons: manufacturing, space, power, people, tools and money."[15]

With production capabilities cut in half and no immediate source of capital, Jack Lewis and Joe Zemke flew to Japan in December 1993 to discuss the future of Amdahl with Fujitsu.

At this meeting, Fujitsu agreed to loan Amdahl up to $100 million.[16] More significantly, however, it was agreed that Fujitsu would be responsible for future mainframe manufacturing, leaving Amdahl responsible for some of the System 390 development, as well as marketing, support, service and systems integration. Only limited engineering and manufacturing of mainframe accessories would now be performed at Amdahl in California. Its manufacturing facility in Ireland would be converted to a software development center. For the company that had spent five years bringing the first non-IBM mainframes to market, this was an earth-shattering development.

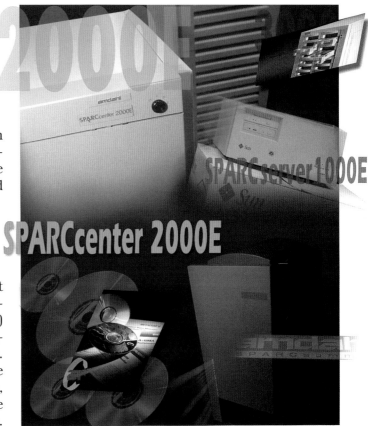

In 1993, Amdahl formed an alliance with Sun Microsystems to sell that company's SPARCcenter server lines.

It was, however, another element in Amdahl's plan. Jack Lewis compared Fujitsu to a brick-and-mortar factory, while Amdahl was the architect:

"It was becoming apparent as technology became more dense that more and more of the system was going onto the chip. As a result, since we were moving to new CMOS technology, the differentiation between our two machines was going to become much less. And the cost for both of us to build separate systems had become prohibitive. We had spent between $500 million and $600 million on the 5995M models. So it became obvious to us that if we could find a way to work more closely together, we could both win.... The economics of the situation was overwhelming."[17]

Lyle Topham, who had been an engineer with Amdahl for 22 years, recalled the reaction among engineers and manufacturing personnel who suddenly found their jobs eliminated.

"It depended upon the individual. Some of them were able to look at it and say, 'It's been a great ride, it was very challenging, it was fun, I'm sad that it's over, but that's life.' And there were others who were very angry."[18]

However, most executives realized that Amdahl had no choice. "It was absolutely the right thing to do," said Amdahl employee Tony DeMory in 1996. "We have not lost any momentum for having done it and probably are more profitable as a result. We had to do it."[19]

A Complete Package for Corporate Customers

Several new alliances and changes were designed to boost Amdahl's Business Solutions Group (BSG), which was formed in 1994 as part of the existing service organization. BSG was a consulting and professional services organization that concentrated on four major business areas: management consulting services, systems integration, applications design and development, and distributed systems management.[20] By 1994, services were Amdahl's second largest business, generating 32 percent of revenues, and BSG was to serve as the nucleus for expanding the consulting and professional services element of that business.[21]

"Wall Street wants to know whether Amdahl can change as the market requires," Zemke said. "The answer is absolutely yes. It will take time, but our business is strengthening."[22]

Even the mainframe market, which had seemed on the verge of collapse only a year before, was showing signs of renewed vigor by the middle of 1994. Many customers were finding that it was more expensive than anticipated to convert from centralized mainframe computing to distributed, client-server networks. A strong global economy didn't hurt, either.[23] "There's a role and a place for the mainframe," said Ollie Nutt, then vice president of corporate marketing. "You may want to refer to it as an enterprise server, but it still has a role in the client-server environment."[24]

Peter Labé, a securities analyst who studied Amdahl for many years and became senior vice president of the Buckingham Research Group, discussed this critical turning point:

"Because of the development of the microprocessor, by 1993 nobody was ordering the mainframe.

Amdahl's popular 5995-1267M 12-way multiprocessor was introduced in 1993.

It was politically incorrect, and that put gigantic pressure on the manufacturers. IBM took billions and billions and billions in write-offs, and Amdahl wrote off millions as well. But guess what? The mainframe wasn't dead. Sometime around the fourth quarter of 1993, people figured out there was going to be room for both.... Amdahl has always stood for excellence and has always done a superior job of putting the customer first, and I don't think that has changed. What has changed are the market conditions, which dictate that if you want to grow, you are going to have to do something different.[25]

Net income for the year saw a gain for the first time since 1990.[26] Amdahl closed 1994 with revenue of $1.6 billion and net income of $74.8 million, a dramatic improvement over the dismal performance of 1993.[27]

The Anniversary

In 1995, the company celebrated the 20th anniversary of its first mainframe shipments. In the two preceding decades, Amdahl had injected real competition into the large-scale computing market, something that no one had thought possible. Accordingly, it was a fitting time to announce the newest generation of Amdahl mainframes, the Millennium series, due for shipment in 1996 and employing the lower-cost CMOS technology.

Fortunately, it appeared the pundits had been wrong. Instead of desktop computers wiping out the market for mainframes, the demand for mainframe CPUs actually increased in the first months of 1995.[28] All Amdahl had to do was hold on long enough to introduce the competitive CMOS technology.

Throughout this period, the company continued to aggressively market its older ECL (emitter-coupled logic) mainframes. In February, Amdahl installed three Model 5995-1267M multiprocessors, the first 12-way multiprocessors in the world, at customer sites in the United States.[29] One customer, United States Fidelity and Guaranty, replaced an older IBM and an older Amdahl mainframe with a single 5995-1267M and found that throughput increased by 19 percent. The company

projected it was going to save $4 million over a three-year period because of the upgrade.[30]

The difficulties inherent in waiting for a new product were compounded by problems in the storage system market. Amdahl was still selling storage processors that had been introduced in 1988, and sales were declining. Newer RAID (redundant arrays of independent disks) storage systems had seriously undermined Amdahl's market share, and there was a need to get the once-successful storage operation back on track.

Greg Grodhaus, a 20-year veteran of Memorex-Telex Corporation, was brought in. A few weeks before his arrival, Amdahl's Spectris RAID Disk Array was announced. This was the long-awaited next-generation storage system for the IBM-compatible data center.[31] The Spectris Array was expected to help regain market share lost to competitors' RAID storage products.[32] In addition, its less expensive technology would allow Amdahl to compete more effectively in a price-sensitive marketplace.

Storage systems sales were also growing to meet the new demands of distributed open systems, and Amdahl's LVS 4500 storage system for the open system market was announced the following year. Among its distinguishing features were performance that improved as capacity grew, complete data availability, and the ability to connect to and support a broad range of open systems platforms, including both UNIX and Windows NT.

To celebrate introduction of the LVS system, code-named Elvis during its development by Amdahl employees, Grodhaus turned the small cafe in the E1 Building into something of a shrine, with Elvis pictures on the walls, Elvis records in a corner jukebox and Elvis videos on a small television set. Checkered tablecloths and an old-fashioned menu completed the fifties look.

Finally, near the end of 1995, the Antares Alliance Group announced the third generation of its ObjectStar software, which extended its usefulness to both UNIX and Windows NT environments as well as MVS platforms.

These three products — the new software, the Millennium and the Spectris storage system — were expected to successfully carry the company through the next year, although company officers

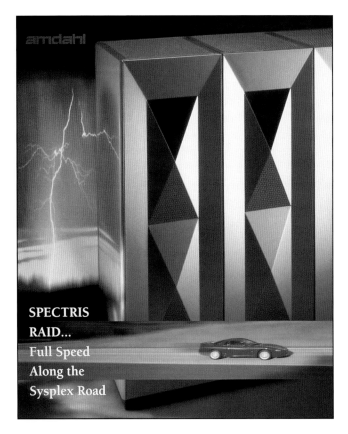

Above: The Spectris RAID Disk Array storage subsystem was introduced in 1995. Heading into the future, Amdahl's product lineup includes mainframes, storage units, front-end servers and consulting services.

Right: Amdahl's storage products were important to open computing systems.

as we enter 1996, of course, is the successful execution of our business plan," they wrote. "Successfully accomplishing that will allow us to emerge strongly from what will likely be a very difficult first half of the year. We should then enjoy reasonable improvement in the second half."[33]

The Business Plan

Despite the company's misgivings about the immediate future, all did not end poorly in 1995. In fact, Amdahl was as upbeat about the future as it could have been, considering the circumstances. For almost three years, company executives had been positioning Amdahl to compete in a new computing environment. They had pushed it toward services and software, even going so far as to cede the manufacture of mainframes to Fujitsu.

Then in late 1995, Amdahl made a move that would forever change the way the company related to its customers and to the business world at large. Over the previous year, Amdahl executives had been involved in negotiations to acquire a Canadian professional services and consulting company called DMR Group, Inc.

In November, Amdahl completed that acquisition and quickly reorganized to accommodate the sudden influx of employees and expertise. The DMR

were very aware of the volatility surrounding Amdahl. In 1995, the company posted a dip in revenue to $1.5 billion from $1.63 billion in 1994. Income dropped even more dramatically, from $74.8 million to $28.5 million.

This decline wasn't due wholly to substandard sales of systems. Mainframe unit sales had held up well throughout most of the year, but prices suddenly plummeted in the fourth quarter when IBM began unloading ECL machines in anticipation of its own CMOS systems. As a result of the price drop, Amdahl was forced to write down $26 million in mainframe inventories.

This was an ominous note on which to end the year, as executives dourly pointed out in the 1995 annual report to shareholders. "The key to success

Group, now including what had been Amdahl's Business Solutions Group, was set up to provide customers with "complete enterprise computing solutions," drawing not only on new service offer-

ings but also on Amdahl's hardware and software products. The Open Enterprise Solutions Group was established to provide server and storage hardware for Unix and Windows NT computing environments. The Antares Alliance Group provided ObjectStar software, while the Enterprise Computing Group maintained Amdahl's traditional focus on System 390 storage products and mainframe processors.

Given the anticipated synergies among all its business units, Zemke and Lewis were able to predict that 1996 would be a good year — despite the expected challenges. Amdahl was truly knitting into a "multifaceted enterprise

computing company," as discussed in the 1995 annual report to shareholders:

"We achieved one of our primary objectives for the year, the expansion of our new businesses, which should continue to grow from a little over 20 percent of revenues in 1995 to approximately 40 percent in 1996. In fostering that growth, we have shifted our revenue mix more heavily toward the services sector, and we have significantly strengthened the ObjectStar technology and distribution channels.... It is also imperative that we effectively leverage the strengths of DMR and capitalize on the synergies that exist among our emerging businesses."[34]

These 1993 posters promoted Amdahl's Open Enterprise Systems.

Based in Montreal, DMR was acquired by Amdahl in late 1995. The company became the cornerstone of Amdahl's consulting and professional services business.

CHAPTER ELEVEN

THE DMR AND TRECOM ACQUISITIONS
1996

"The only way you are going to make money is to engage the customer in consulting and services. Twenty years ago you would just sell hardware; now you really have to be a strategic partner to the customer."

— Alan Bell, 1996[1]

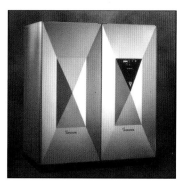

I N MANY WAYS, 1996 HERALDED a watershed year for the "new" Amdahl. With the purchase of DMR in late 1995, Amdahl had put in motion powerful forces of change that would only accelerate in the coming months. True to predictions, however, the year posed some major challenges.

As competition to IBM, Amdahl had survived admirably in the cut-throat world of mainframe manufacturing. By the mid-1990s, however, the company was branching out on its own. Customer information processing needs, previously characterized by large data centers filled with humming mainframes, had broadened to include servers that distributed information over client/server networks to intelligent desktop machines. This increased complexity put a premium on services that helped customers cope with the many kinds of machines and operating systems they were suddenly confronting.

The Business Solutions Group (BSG) had been formed in 1994 with exactly this need in mind. Led by Michael J. Poehner, who joined the company in 1992 as a general manager in charge of services and product sales for the Eastern United States, BSG planned to grow through acquisition. "The Business Solutions Group really didn't have the infrastructure, support, reputation, tools or methodologies that you need to run such a busi-

ness," Poehner explained. "We knew right away we were going to have to acquire something."[2]

Poehner had risen through IBM's management ranks between 1974 and 1987, joining Amdahl after gaining additional experience at Businessland and Zenith Data Systems.[3] In his position as worldwide general manager of the Business Solutions Group, Poehner's primary responsibility was to expand the new organization. After preliminary searches, evaluations and analysis, Amdahl came across DMR Group, Inc., "a jewel of a company" in Canada that fit perfectly with Amdahl's game plan.[4]

The DMR Story

In February 1973, three IBM branch managers — Pierre Ducros, Serge Meilleur and Alain Roy — decided to break free of Big Blue's bureaucratic obstacles and start a business of their own. With experience in financial services, manufacturing and distribution, and government services, respectively, the executives created a service firm offering the best in professional consulting.

The new Millennium CMOS mainframes were unveiled in 1995 as the fastest large-scale mainframes on the market.

DMR founders, left to right, Pierre Ducros, Alain Roy and Serge Meilleur. The company was named for their initials.

The company, named DMR for its three founders' initials, grew steadily throughout the seventies by focusing on consulting services and avoiding the pitfalls of diversification.

In 1976, DMR managed the complicated scoring system at the Summer Olympic Games in Montreal. The prestigious assignment was repeated at the Olympic Games in Moscow in 1980 and Los Angeles in 1984. DMR successfully leveraged those contracts into a worldwide presence, expanding into Europe, Australia and Asia/Pacific.

DMR consultants were sought-after as a source of senior-level strategic advice, and the company excelled in such disciplines as benefits management, systems integration, and the outsourcing of applications software development and management.

Targeting medium-sized and large companies, DMR's client list included such diverse customers as John Hancock Financial, Microsoft, Sears Roebuck, the Oregon Department of Transportation and Qantas Airways. According to Amdahl, DMR was on a professional level with such giants such as EDS Canada, Andersen Consulting and IBM Canada.[5]

By 1995, DMR employed 2,800 people and boasted revenues in excess of $200 million.[6] The

November 1995 — Amdahl completes acquisition of DMR Group, Inc., a renowned information services consulting firm.

January 1996 — Operating Council is established to integrate the new business. David Wright is promoted from vice president of field operations to executive vice president of Amdahl Systems Group.

March 1996 — President and CEO Joe Zemke retires. Jack Lewis postpones his retirement to again become CEO of Amdahl.

company was listed as one of the world's premier information-technology advisors in the Gartner Group's 1995 list of "Leading Worldwide Professional Services Organizations." Perhaps more importantly, customers in Canada ranked the company first in information-technology services.

In November 1994, however, DMR's founders conducted an in-depth study of the company, its competition and the marketplace and concluded it was time to find a partner. As competition grew in Canada, England and France, the company needed more capital in order to access new markets. In addition, stronger financial capabilities would help the company bid on larger projects. Faced with these circumstances, DMR entered 1995 looking for "a big brother."

The Bidding War

During the summer of 1995, senior management at Amdahl and DMR held a series of meetings to discuss acquisition possibilities. Amdahl's chief financial officer, Bruce Ryan, and Michael Poehner led Amdahl's team, while Pierre Ducros and Michael Auclair represented DMR.[7] In an interview, Poehner elaborated on why Amdahl was interested in DMR:

"They are the premier services company in Canada, and they enjoy the same level of reputation in Australia. They did not have a big presence in the United States, but they had some very significant customers: good relationship with Boeing, good relationship with Visa, good relationship with Sears, and half a dozen of that ilk. Our Business Solutions Group had a little bit of business in France and in Belgium. Almost nothing in the United Kingdom. We had grown the BSG business up to about $75 million in U.S. dollars, and the DMR business was about $220 million. And the BSG business happened to be in places where DMR wasn't. It was a phenomenal match."[8]

From the beginning, it was obvious the two companies were perfect for each other. Amdahl's Business Solutions Group operated in regions that DMR was eager to penetrate. And both DMR and Amdahl were eager to expand in the rapidly growing applications outsourcing business.[9]

Pierre Ducros, DMR's chairman, president and chief executive officer, recalled that the companies' cultures also fit well together:

April 1996 — Amdahl negotiates the purchase of TRECOM Business Systems, Inc., another information services consulting firm. This purchase makes Amdahl one of the world's larger consulting and professional services firms.

December 1996 — The company opens a Business Solutions Centre for Year-2000 conversion services in Montreal.

July 1996 — Mondex International is created to advance a software and chip "smart card" technology for financial transactions.

December 1996 — As the year ends, Amdahl's integration of two new companies and movement into information consulting services are in full swing.

"Amdahl had a philosophy that was much more in sync with what we wanted to do. Amdahl was saying that it knew a lot about hardware and software products, but very little about service. So it asked us to take the lead in service. No arrogance whatsoever. It was really a partnership that was being established, and we liked that."[10]

Amdahl's product-oriented approach to the marketplace also complemented DMR's service approach. DMR's proprietary methods and extensive business processes could be enhanced by Amdahl's software products for open systems management and applications development.[11] In addition, Ducros and Auclair were attracted by Amdahl's ability to supply financial backing.

During negotiations, a plan was established in which DMR would be the focal point of service

operations, and Amdahl's existing Business Solutions Group would be integrated into DMR's established infrastructure.[12]

The acquisition quickly got under way. DMR, like many Canadian companies, had two classes of stock, with closely held Class B shares carrying ten times the voting rights of each of the Class A shares, which were traded on the open market.[13]

On September 13, 1995, Amdahl announced it had secured the right to purchase all of the Class B shares belonging to DMR's three largest shareholders: Pierre Ducros, Alain Roy, and the Ontario Teachers' Pension Board. The price was to be U.S. $8.25 per share, substantially higher than the current market price of approximately U.S. $5.[14] It briefly appeared this commitment would be sufficient to give Amdahl control of the company, allowing it to buy the remaining Class A and B shares, also at $8.25 per share.[15]

The acquisition was almost derailed, however, when a third party, BDM International, Inc., touched off a bidding war. The Virginia-based professional services firm had hired a Montreal attorney to scan DMR's charter, seeking a loophole that would make a competing bid possible. The attorney discovered a 1991 "coattail provision" designed to protect Class A shareholders in the event of a takeover. According to Poehner, BDM bought a few Class A shares and then sued, claiming the provision allowed Class A shares to be converted into Class B shares during a takeover. That would increase the voting rights of current Class A shareholders tenfold and take away the controlling interest Amdahl felt it had secured through the agreement with DMR's three principal stockholders.[16] BDM then made a bid of $9.25 per share.[17]

The Quebec Superior Court reviewed the case and in October ruled in favor of BDM International. Full conversion of Class A to Class B stock would give existing Class A shareholders a huge increase in votes, so the ruling meant Amdahl controlled only 36 percent of the votes and that 64 percent of DMR was still up for grabs. Immediately after the court's decision, Ontario-based IBM Canada,

The LVS 4000 storage system inspired an Elvis-themed cafe in Amdahl, complete with posters and a jukebox.

Your competitors are finding new ways to use I.T. as a competitive tool. Are you keeping up?

P a r a d i g m   S h i f t

LVS 4500

amdahl

The LVS 4500 storage system, referred to as Elvis inside the company, signaled that Amdahl was ready to rejuvenate its storage products. The company was steadily expanding its offerings to include a complete line of large-scale and midrange computing hardware.

Limited, entered the fray, offering U.S. $11 per share.[18] The bidding war had escalated. "We could have realized a profit by selling our 36 percent at $11 if we wanted to," recalled Poehner, "but we did not want that. We wanted the company."[19]

And DMR wanted to be a part of Amdahl. The company's founders did not believe BDM International would have been a suitable fit,[20] and the former IBMers perceived Big Blue as having very different values and methods of operation.[21] Jacques Pigeon, a DMR vice president, said he had been impressed with Amdahl throughout the negotiations. "I really liked the attitude and the quality of the people I met. I liked their ethics, the way they approached us, their attitudes and

their values. We appreciated Amdahl's approach that a customer problem is an Amdahl problem."[22]

Amdahl had already positioned a transition staff in DMR's Montreal headquarters, but the court ruling brought the acquisition process to a screeching halt.[23] With IBM's bid of U.S. $11.00, BDM International dropped out of the picture, and the next move would have to be made by Amdahl.

After much planning, Amdahl executives developed a clever strategy for besting its longtime competitor and securing DMR. The company announced that it was appealing the decision of the Quebec Superior Court with a hearing scheduled for November 20. Directly and indirectly, executives made it known that they expected the ruling to be in their favor. By doing this, Amdahl discouraged seven arbitrage firms in New York that had accumulated roughly a third of DMR's stock. If the court ruled in Amdahl's favor, those firms would receive only Amdahl's original offer of U.S. $8.25 per share. On October 31, 1995, the day after IBM's board of directors approved its

An internal advertisement for Amdahl's capacity management solutions highlights the company's storage options.

U.S. $11.00-per-share bid, Amdahl delivered letters to the arbitragers raising its offer to U.S. $12.00 but stating that the offer would expire at the close of the business day.

Those firms quickly contacted IBM officials to see if the company would increase its offer. The answer was yes, but the arbitragers would have to wait a few days until IBM's board could approve a new offer, exactly what Amdahl had hoped. Amdahl executives remained firm, advising arbitragers to either accept the new offer or wait another month for the court to settle the matter. The firms asked Amdahl to raise the offer to U.S. $12.50 per share, the price at which DMR stock was trading that day. Amdahl agreed, as long as the company received enough shares from the firms to secure majority ownership of DMR. Fifteen minutes before the market closed, all seven arbitrage firms agreed to sell all their DMR stock at U.S. $12.50 per share. For a total cost of about $150 million, including expenses, Amdahl completed the acquisition of DMR in November 1995.[24]

Joining Forces

Although DMR and Amdahl shared similar corporate values, the cultural and language differences presented some problems. To help get the marriage off to a good start, Amdahl hired Dallas-based Pritchett and Associates, Inc., a firm with two decades of experience in managing mergers and acquisitions.[25] Coordinating the effort for Amdahl was John Lutalah, whose financial background, knowledge of Amdahl and fluency in French made him exceptionally qualified for the task.[26] Lutalah worked closely with Michael Poehner, who became president of the combined operation. Pierre Ducros, chairman and CEO of DMR, led the transition process for DMR.[27]

As with any acquisition, it was important to move quickly, explained Price Pritchett, CEO of Pritchett and Associates. "When a merger hits, you've got a generic set of problems that start. They are always there, and you cannot prevent them. There are going to be communication problems, productivity downturn, power struggles, and a loss of team play, job satisfaction and job commitment. You can only anticipate the fact that they're going to be there and just try to minimize the impact."[28]

After an initial briefing attended by more than a dozen of Amdahl's top department leaders, Pritchard and Associates sent out a standard Merger Management Review so Amdahl could assess the leadership and technical abilities of DMR staff. Unfortunately, the questionnaires were written in English, creating a mild uproar in Quebec, where DMR's headquarters and many of its employees were located. Many of those employees did not appreciate being questioned or tested in anything but French, their native language. Although the

review was quickly withdrawn, the incident revealed some resentment among a few key DMR employees who had hoped the company would be sold to another French-Canadian firm.

A few weeks after the acquisition, cofounder Serge Meilleur and four other senior executives left DMR to form another company, also specializing in information-technology consulting services.[29]

Within a few months, however, early concerns and questions associated with the merger had been addressed, and Amdahl was ready to take another big step in expanding the services sector of its business.

A Sudden Departure

Three months following the DMR acquisition, in early 1996, President and CEO Joe Zemke unexpectedly retired from Amdahl for personal reasons. The news stunned industry analysts and even company insiders. Jack Lewis, who was about to retire, returned to the position he had held between 1983 and 1992. He gave a simple and eloquent response to the announcement: "Joe Zemke has positioned the company well to take advantage of the dynamic markets that we are now able to address. We are grateful for his many contributions."[30]

TRECOM Business Systems, Inc.

With DMR successfully in the Amdahl family, the company next turned its attention to another consulting and professional services firm, TRECOM Business Systems, Inc. Founded in Edison, New Jersey, in 1985 by Frank Casagrande and Manny Arturi, experts in the business and technology consulting field, TRECOM began as a firm that provided personnel for information systems projects.

TRECOM was Casagrande's third information consulting startup firm:

"I had been in the business since 1957 and had my own companies since 1965. I'd seen the

Joe Zemke, right, announced his retirement in 1996. Jack Lewis, although he was preparing to retire, once again took the top position at Amdahl.

demand for business solutions based on technology growing at an ever-expanding rate. There was a need for people that understood business and understood technology to talk to clients, to offer them solutions that would enhance their business."[31]

In the first five years of its existence, TRECOM slowly shifted its focus from supplying personnel to project management, allowing the company to be "in step" with its clients' information needs and goals. The company expanded its professional service offerings to include systems design, development and integration, data warehousing, document imaging, application portfolio management, and Year-2000 software date conversion.[32]

TRECOM methods also were used by *Fortune* 100 companies to reengineer centralized systems and create corporate client/server networks.[33] By the end of 1995, TRECOM had become one of the fastest-growing professional services companies in the United States, with 1,700 employees and annual revenues of $140 million.[34] Since 1993, the annual revenue growth rate had exceeded 40 percent.[35]

Company officers, however, were eager to embrace new customers and markets. To do so, TRECOM needed more financial backing. As Casagrande remembered, "We were just getting bigger and bigger. The only thing that was holding us back was money, and we were gobbling up that money very fast."[36]

As a privately held company, TRECOM had the options of going public, getting itself acquired or seeking private investment to raise the necessary finances.[37] After looking at what it was trying to accomplish, TRECOM officers decided that acquisition was the best route, with a public offering running second. In terms of a match, Casagrande said they were originally looking for a European company with no base in the United States, a company that would fund TRECOM with little oversight. When their investment banker recommended Amdahl, Casagrande said the match was even better:

"When Amdahl came along, it was perfect. It was the right size company in our minds, doing a billion and a half in sales. We weren't really interested in a big company like an IBM, because in a

big company like that, we would have been close to a zero."[38]

Fortunately, Amdahl did not have to engage in a bidding war in this acquisition. On April 3, 1996, Amdahl announced it had acquired TRECOM for $140 million.[39] The transition went smoothly, and by mid-1996, a new organization, known internationally as the DMR Consulting Group and, initially, as DMR-TRECOM in the United States, was formed to offer customers a very broad range of professional consulting services. The TRECOM name was dropped entirely in 1998.

As foreseen, the three companies had synergistic strengths.[40] TRECOM offices were concentrated in the Eastern half of the United States, from New Jersey to Texas,[41] and this presence would help Amdahl and DMR expand into the rich Northeastern sector — the largest computer consulting market in the world.[42] TRECOM's customer base also complemented Amdahl's existing customer base. Sixty-five percent of TRECOM's business was in the telecommunications industry,[43] with an additional strong presence in the financial services sector, both of which were long-time major markets for Amdahl.[44] Robert Sargenti, chief operating officer for the DMR Consulting Group worldwide, explained the importance of telecommunications in the new organization's future:

"There is so much convergence going on in the telecommunications industry in this country that it's still our number one customer and will be for some time. Telephone companies, which used to be government-owned entities, are now being privatized, and that creates a whole new set of circumstances. It's been very, very positive for us."[45]

DMR's methodical marketing approach, based on broad technological expertise and spanning many industries, contrasted with TRECOM's aggressive marketing approach geared to such specific industries as telecommunications.[46] "TRECOM's strategy has been to market its services vertically, building a high level of expertise in selected industries," said TRECOM cofounder Manny Arturi, who was the company's president and chief operating officer. "As a result, we have created an impressive portfolio of proven, stan-

dardized solutions for needs common within those industries."[47]

On a broader scale, Amdahl's professional services business was being further fueled by increasing demands for Year-2000 software conversion services. The challenge facing corporations, banks, on-line service firms, government agencies and other users of management information systems was how to modify computer applications to recognize the year 2000.

In what proved to be a monstrously expensive oversight, early computer programmers decided to save precious memory space by identifying calendar years by only the last two digits and assuming the first two numbers to be one and nine. As the millennium approached, this created a major international problem. If the computer code was not changed, many date-based systems for things such as stock transactions, insurance, and mortgages would identify dates in the year 2000 and beyond as still being in the 1900s, basically turning the clock back 100 years.

As a result, billions of lines of code had to be edited before the millennium arrived, and accomplishing that goal was an expensive and time-consuming challenge unparalleled in the short

Amdahl's information consulting group was reinforced with the acquisition of TRECOM. Pictured are the company's founders, left to right, Tom Burke, Russ Powell, Dick Hourihan, Frank Casagrande and Manny Arturi.

history of computing. As a hypothetical example, if a software program consisting of 10 million lines of code contained one date reference every 25 lines, it would take one programmer roughly 20 years to make the necessary changes.[48]

Amdahl was well prepared for the challenge, as Year-2000 conversions had already been a primary strategic objective at TRECOM, which had more than 400 employees working specifically on such projects in its 30,000-square-foot Business Solutions Center in Jersey City, New Jersey.[49] DMR's Montreal office also opened a Business Solutions Centre for Year-2000 services in December 1996, expanding the company's office space from 1,700 to 10,000 square feet and securing contracts with such premier clients as AT&T Canada, the Province of Quebec, M&M Mars, the National Bank of Canada, and AXA Insurance.[50] By the end of 1996, the company had a huge backlog of Year-2000 conversion contracts.

The SmartCard Group

Also in 1996, Amdahl formed the SmartCard Group, with Vice President Chuck Fonner as general manager. The group's assignment was to build infrastructure for the fast-growing electronic cash (e-cash) market around the world. The systems would support an advanced chip and software technology called Mondex Global Electronic Cash Program, developed by the world's largest banks, which keeps track of financial transactions through the use of a plastic card. It can be used via telephones or automatic teller machines for electronic cash transfers and shopping transactions. Mondex International, Limited, formed in July 1996, is owned by 17 major banking organizations on four continents and is headquartered in London. Amdahl is offering a turnkey package with the capacity to grow and change with the bank's requirements. The system uses a wide range of products, from ObjectStar software to LVS 4500 storage systems, according to Fonner:

Above: With its SmartCard Group, Amdahl moved into the electronic cash market. The system allowed over-the-phone and ATM banking transactions.

Right: As the year wound down, Amdahl was a radically changed company, except for its historical insistence on high quality and excellent service.

"We are the only vendor right now that has a complete system. This is the best example of what happens when you take all of Amdahl's products and put them together."[51]

New Organization — New Growth

As the 1996 annual report noted, "Even though 1996 was a difficult year financially for Amdahl Corporation, it was also a year of sweeping change and significant progress toward the achievement of long-range strategic goals."[52]

With the acquisitions of DMR and TRECOM, Amdahl's professional services business grew nearly fourfold in 1996.[53] By the end of the year, revenues from all of its service and software businesses exceeded $1 billion, more than double its hardware sales. Moreover, the acquisitions nearly doubled Amdahl's total employment, from around 5,200 to more than 10,000, with 60 percent of the workforce devoted to service and software.

Within a short time, Amdahl had significantly altered its business, but it wasn't venturing into

completely foreign waters. Although the revenue mix had changed dramatically, Amdahl's strategic focus remained firmly on the customer. As noted in the company's 1996 annual report:

"Amdahl is in the business of helping customers gain competitive advantage from information systems. It is a challenging and exciting business to be in because all our customers share the challenge of change. All must constantly anticipate and respond to change in their industries and markets, so we are there with them anticipating and responding to their changing needs. To succeed in such dynamic times requires business agility grounded on a solid strategy."[54]

Taking Charge Again

Success also required flexibility and the ability to assimilate all the company's new endeavors into its business plan. Amdahl created an Operating Council to integrate daily operations of the company's diverse businesses, including the two new acquisitions, and to cut costs by recentralizing product development and support functions such as marketing. At the same time, David Wright was promoted from vice president of field operations to executive vice president in charge of the newly created Amdahl Systems Group. In this position, Wright was responsible for Amdahl's mainframe and data storage products, product maintenance and the field sales organization.

Reducing operating costs for both marketing and product development served to ease the financial squeeze, while the growing service business continued to earn profits. Neither, however, could offset the negative impact as Amdahl struggled through the final months of its transition to the new Millennium family of CMOS mainframes.

As customers either postponed buying decisions entirely or insisted on deeply discounted prices for the remaining inventory of 5995M ECL mainframes, hardware sales fell off dramatically and losses mounted. The first Millennium processors weren't shipped until November.

Amdahl posted a net loss of $313 million for the year on revenue of $1.6 billion. A large part of that was attributable to "paper" transactions, including a $130 million write-off of its older, outmoded ECL mainframes and another $20.7 million write-off of in-process research and development associated with the TRECOM acquisition.[55] Competitors, meanwhile, were winning business from Amdahl by cautioning customers that current financial woes could persist and eventually put the company out of business.

Lewis began looking for a solution:

"It became apparent to me that the right solution over an extended period of time was to make Amdahl and Fujitsu even closer so that we could take advantage of their tremendous size and resources in a much more direct way. I felt that for the best interests of our customers and our employees and our shareholders, we should put together something with Fujitsu."[56]

The main building of Fujitsu Research & Manufacturing, based in Kawasaki, Japan. Fujitsu negotiated to buy Amdahl in 1997.

CHAPTER TWELVE

COMING FULL CIRCLE
1997–2000

"If we can tie Fujitsu much closer to our R&D, take advantage of their financial strength, and combine that with our company, our people and our ability to get to the customer, we could really make a big impact in the industry."

— CEO David Wright[1]

ONE OF AMDAHL'S TRAditional strengths has always been adaptability. Over its lifetime, the company continually refined its focus and product mix as the computer and information processing industry evolved. In 1997, the company was again able to adapt to monumental change — even as it successfully completed its transition into an information services company and derived about two-thirds of its revenue from that piece of its business.

Jack Lewis, Amdahl's long-time guiding influence, began early in the year to orchestrate a deal that would change Amdahl forever. He approached Fujitsu with the prospect of a merger. At first, Fujitsu saw no benefit to changing a successful business relationship that dated back 25 years. But Lewis convinced Fujitsu executives that the merger would be a good way to give Amdahl long-term viability in the marketplace, as well as a good way for Fujitsu to strengthen its position in the North American market. With shareholder approval, Amdahl officers were ready in July 1997 to make the stunning announcement that Amdahl would become a wholly owned subsidiary of the Japanese computer giant.

As Lewis had predicted, the acquisition boasted long-range synergies for both companies, with Amdahl benefiting from Fujitsu's financial strength and technological expertise and Fujitsu gaining access to Amdahl's customers and expanding its global reach to the North American market.

As the deal was finalized, Lewis made another surprise announcement. He was retiring from the company he had led as either president or chairman for 20 years. David B. Wright, executive vice president of the Amdahl Systems Group, would rise to the position of CEO. In an interview shortly after the news broke, Lewis looked back over the breadth of his long career with Amdahl:

"When I look back on it, I'd say we're a company that made a difference. We changed the way people thought about purchasing their data processing equipment. We were the first ones to successfully take on IBM in the heartland of their business. We were able to establish the thought process that people could buy from a multitude of vendors. I think we developed an attitude and approach to customer service that is the best of anyone in our industry. We've made the whole industry better. We built a company that has great employees, a tremendous amount of esprit de corps, a tremendous can-do attitude, and I'm proud to have been

With the acquisition complete, Amdahl operated as a subsidiary of Fujitsu. A new, more modern logo was introduced in the late 1990s.

Above: The Fuji Electric Company building, pictured in 1935.

Opposite page: Fujitsu began manufacturing communication equipment in 1953.

associated with all those people over the past 20 years.

"I've spent my time and done the best that I could do, and it's time for me to turn the reins over to a younger group of managers and let them take what we've built and grow it. I'd be glad to do anything I can to help them, but like all parents, I suspect I'll find the kids get pretty independent."[2]

Lewis would be called upon to continue helping his company, but in the role of "elder statesman" as chairman of Amdahl's new board of directors.

Fujitsu

When Amdahl became part of Fujitsu, it joined one of the world's largest and best established computer companies. Fujitsu was founded in 1935 from the communications division of Fuji Electric Company, Limited, which built punch-card machines for the Japanese census.[3] The young Fujitsu was spun off as a telecommunications enterprise in partnership with Siemens, a European company. The word "Fujitsu" itself is derived from "fu," which comes from Furukawa Electric, the parent company of Fuji, "ji," derived from the Japanese pro-

July 1997 — Amdahl agrees to be purchased by long-time partner Fujitsu.

July 1997 — Amdahl posts a profit in its last quarter as a public company.

August 1997 — CEO Jack Lewis retires and David Wright becomes Amdahl's new CEO.

nunciation of Siemens, an original partner, and "*tsu*," which is short for "*tsushin*," the Japanese word for telecommunications.

The same year it was founded, Fujitsu introduced Japan's first commercial digital calculator,[4] but its real expertise lay in telephone switching systems and electromechanical equipment. By

1945, the Fuji-type telephone had been adopted by the Teishinin, or the current Ministry of Postal Service, and in 1949, a growing Fujitsu was listed on the Tokyo Stock Exchange.

These were hard years for all of Japan, as World War II had a devastating impact on Japanese industry. After the war, the government reevaluated what role Japan should play on the world stage and developed a policy of economic assistance that continues to this day to protect industries that could expand and strengthen the nation.[5] Electronics is among these industries, considered ideal for a nation with limited natural resources.[6] This government support was initiated at a time when a new market began to emerge for an innovative device called the computer.

Recognizing Opportunity

Fujitsu President Kanjiro Okada decided in the early 1950s that Fujitsu must begin serious research to create a commercially successful computer, and he knew who would lead the effort: "We have a tremendous genius on board," Okada said. "So let's use Dr. Ikeda as the focus of a project which will generate a computer."[7]

May 1998 — The companies introduce their first joint venture, the *team*server family of products, which is capable of integrating many operating systems.

Fall 1998 — The Amdahl Integrated Information Suite is introduced to revive the company's storage division. It is built around the LVS 4600 open system storage unit and the Spectris Platinum RAID-1 server.

Summer 1998 — Amdahl begins shipping the Millennium 700 series mainframe, which is introduced as the fastest mainframe on the market.

Winter 1998 — Amdahl, combined with Fujitsu, has made its successful transition into a full-service provider of information delivery systems, including hardware, software and support.

Dr. Toshio Ikeda had joined Fujitsu in 1946 as a bright 23-year-old graduate of the Tokyo Institute of Technology. Described as a "big man with a booming voice, Dr. Ikeda was considered by many to be a true genius."[8] He began his career designing telephone switching systems before he was chosen to lead Fujitsu's computer development project in the early 1950s. He would later play a prominent role not only in guiding Fujitsu into the computer market, but in establishing a relationship with the American computer whiz Gene Amdahl.

During the 1950s, research in Japan was primarily conducted in large government laboratories and through industry collaboration. The Ministry of International Trade and Industry (MITI) operated the Electrotechnical Laboratory (ETL), where Fujitsu engineers collaborated with researchers who had been working on a relay-based computer. The company also resumed its technical cooperation with Siemens.

The result in 1954 was Japan's first commercially available computer, the Fujitsu FACOM 100, a nonprogrammable computer designed for accounting applications. Its construction, reflecting Fujitsu's creative adaption of telecommunications technology, was based on a series of hardwired electromagnetic relay switches adapted from telephone switching equipment. Fujitsu built only eight such relay-based systems by the end of the decade.

Japan's computer manufacturers were unable to meet the growing demand for computers, and 90 percent of new computers came from foreign manufacturers through the early sixties. In the

Right: In 1954, Fujitsu introduced the FACOM 100, Japan's first commercial computer.

Below: The FACOM 100 was a transistor-based machine. A 1950s transistor assembly is pictured.

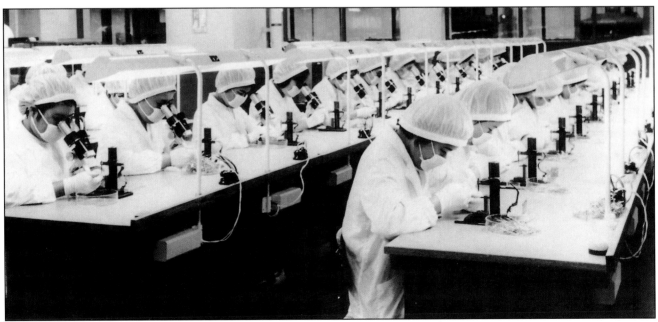

United States, digital computer production had already become a $300 million a year industry.[9] Despite the technology gap, Fujitsu recognized the potential and aggressively pursued it. The company began volume production of transistors in 1960, reorganized itself into individual communications and electronics groups in 1961 and founded Fujitsu Laboratories, a research group, the following year.

By 1963, Fujitsu was technologically superior to its Japanese rivals and was awarded the leading role in the FONTAC project. Supported by MITI, the FONTAC project challenged Japanese electronics companies to create a large-scale, transistor-based computer that could be connected to smaller satellite computers.[10] The end result was the Fujitsu 250, released commercially in 1965 as the FACOM 230-50.

Its architecture would serve as the basis for Fujitsu large-scale general-purpose computers, as well as for the FACOM 270 family of scientific computers, until the end of the 1970s.[11] The transistor-based FACOM 230 series was accepted immediately by Japanese banks and universities, and Fujitsu began exporting computers to the Philippines, its first overseas market.

In 1966, Fujitsu began volume production of integrated circuits and unveiled Japan's first mainframe based on integrated-circuit technology and equipped with its own operating system. The company established its first U.S. office in New York in 1967, and its product line grew to include communications equipment, computer peripherals, data processing services and office equipment.

In the late 1960s, however, Fujitsu lost a major contract to Hitachi because the Fujitsu mainframe

Above: Pictured from left to right are Takuma Yamamoto, Kanjiro Okada and Toshio Ikeda. These men were instrumental in supporting Gene Amdahl.

Below: By the 1960s, Fujitsu had introduced the FACOM 230 series of mainframes, which became Japan's leading large-system computers.

wasn't compatible with IBM's operating system software. The loss spurred Ikeda to persuade Fujitsu's management that competitiveness was linked to IBM compatibility in certain parts of the world.

In 1968, Ikeda met Gene Amdahl and became "instantly enamored" with the fellow innovator.[12] He was aware of Amdahl's expertise in the area of compatibility, and when Dr. Amdahl began his search for investors a few years later, the Fujitsu-Amdahl relationship was born. Future Fujitsu President Takuma Yamamoto accompanied Ikeda

Driven by FACOM sales, Fujitsu began a transition from a communications company to primarily a computer maker. The FACOM M200, bottom, is pictured with a 9450 terminal (below).

to Sunnyvale, California, in early 1971 to hear Amdahl's proposal.

Despite sharp discussions among Fujitsu's management about such a large investment in a company without a product, the companies ultimately agreed to challenge IBM in the compatible mainframe market. Ikeda, Amdahl's chief supporter, would not see the relationship bear fruit, however. In late 1974, he collapsed in Tokyo's International Airport and died a few days later. Japan and the computer industry had lost a gifted and remarkable man who, Yamamoto recalled, "more than anyone else is the true father of Fujitsu computers."[13]

Fujitsu's early investments in both computer and semiconductor research were rewarded during the mid-1970s. The commitment to the computer market was most evident when compared to Fujitsu's competitors. Seventy-two percent of the company's revenues came from computer sales. The figure at rival NEC was only 25 percent, and only 6 percent at Hitachi and Toshiba.[14] In the semiconductor arena, Fujitsu would come to dominate the memory chip market.

Fujitsu's success during this period can be attributed in part to a strategy that originated with the company's investment in Amdahl Corporation.

When Fujitsu could not develop certain technologies or gain access to them through licensing agreements, it simply bought into companies that could meet its needs. Fujitsu's relationship with Amdahl Corporation helped secure technology and the knowledge needed to successfully compete in the compatible mainframe market. At the same time, Amdahl received from Fujitsu venture financing, access to world-class semiconductors and engineering assistance.

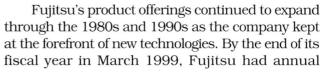

Fujitsu's product offerings continued to expand through the 1980s and 1990s as the company kept at the forefront of new technologies. By the end of its fiscal year in March 1999, Fujitsu had annual sales of $43.3 billion and more than 188,000 employees working in approximately 100 countries.[15]

A Closer Relationship

This kind of global presence could only help Amdahl as it joined with Fujitsu, and the relationship between the two companies was even familial, said Jack Lewis:

"I gave a talk to our employees when we announced this transaction. I told them, in some respects, it's like what happened with my children. I was there at their birth and raised them through adolescence, their teen years, and they got to be adults and went off to college. And some of them moved back home. Fujitsu was here at the birth, and they helped us all the way through our adolescence and teen years and now we've moved back home again. We're part of the family, and Fujitsu views us as that."[16]

Part of the family, perhaps, but the new CEO, David Wright, had a significant challenge. The company was in the midst of a major shift in corporate strategy and was working to clearly articulate its strategy to the world. The acquisitions of DMR and TRECOM had transformed Amdahl into a consulting and services company, yet its roots were firmly in large-scale computing. Significantly, at the time of the merger with Fujitsu, Amdahl's new Millennium CMOS mainframe was beginning to have an impact on the marketplace, allowing

Above: Jack Lewis announced his retirement in 1997 after 20 years at upper management in Amdahl.

Left: The Millennium 830 was introduced as the fastest and most powerful mainframe on the market. Amdahl remains the world's second-largest mainframe manufacturer.

the company to report a small profit in its last reporting period as a public company, the second quarter of 1997.

Wright began his mission by seeking synergies with Amdahl's much larger partner — and he didn't have to look far. The companies were already old partners, and Fujitsu had always held a major stake in Amdahl. As Wright explained:

"If we could take advantage of Fujitsu's financial strength and combine that with our company, our people and our ability to get to the customer, we could really make a big impact in the industry. This merger was never a transaction that was done to change the make-up of Amdahl or change our culture. At the time, Fujitsu owned 42 percent of us, and what we told them was, 'Move forward and

take the balance of the company, and then let's talk about our common goals.' And Fujitsu's common goals are very close to ours. They want to become much more global and they want to grow market share profitably. What became evident to them is that the best way to do that is through Amdahl, which has one of the best sales and support channels in the world."[17]

Above: David Wright became the new CEO of Amdahl in 1997. Under his direction, Amdahl reorganized to address the whole spectrum of needs for large-scale computing environments.

Below: A poster promoting the NT Server that Amdahl introduced in 1996. Amdahl accelerated its move into the NT-server market.

"The combination of Fujitsu's superior technologies and Amdahl's marketing support, consulting capabilities and customer relationships will enhance Fujitsu's presence in the U.S. and Europe in the high-growth areas of information-technology products and services," confirmed Kazuto Kojima, a member of Fujitsu's board of directors and general manager of the marketing and computer groups.

Just as Amdahl broadens the distribution of Fujitsu products in those geographic areas and in industry sectors, such as telecommunications and financial services, where Amdahl is particularly strong, Fujitsu and its subsidiaries provide new distribution channels for Amdahl in Asia and Latin America. Shortly after the merger, the marketing information databases of Amdahl, Fujitsu and other Fujitsu subsidiaries were integrated.

In May 1998, the first joint product was introduced. Called the *team*server, this family of Windows NT servers was aimed at the integrated data center where large OS/390 mainframes work in tandem with several different operating systems, including the ubiquitous Windows NT, in a multi-tiered structure. The *team*server is built by Fujitsu and marketed by both Fujitsu and Amdahl.

New Mainframes and Storage Offerings

In 1998, Amdahl also began to ship the Millennium 700 series, hailed at the time by *InformationWEEK* magazine as the "fastest CMOS-based mainframes available."[18] Operating at a speed of 80 MIPS per single processor, the 700 series used up to 12 processors but required only a fraction of the space that older emitter-coupled-logic (ECL) machines needed. In introducing the Millennium 700, Amdahl brought to market the first OS/390-compatible CMOS processor capable of replacing the largest ECL mainframes. Among the first companies to install a 700 was the Southern Company, a large independent U.S. power producer. Before long, Millennium 700 mainframes

had also been installed in Great Britain, France, Belgium, Germany and Canada.

However, in a pattern by now familiar to the fast-moving world of mainframe technology, an IBM CMOS mainframe was unveiled later in 1998 with slightly greater capacity, which Amdahl again countered in December 1998 with the new Millennium 800 models.

In the storage business, Amdahl announced the Amdahl Integrated Information Suite, built around two new storage products: the LVS 4600 open system storage device and the Spectris Platinum RAID-1 system that offers OS/390 compatibility. The LVS 4600 supports the Unix and Windows NT operating systems, while Spectris Platinum was designed for the System 390 data

The LVS 4600 was introduced in 1998 as part of a comprehensive suite of storage products.

center. It is anticipated that future generations will be able to support all three computing environments with a single product offering.

Total Solutions Strategy Gains Momentum

These new hardware products made up only part of the global strategy that company officers had clearly articulated by 1999: to become the premier provider of complete computing solutions for large-scale IT users. Unlike competitors that addressed pieces of a corporate computing issue, Amdahl had the capability and expertise to design system-wide information technology platforms and software for huge operations such as financial services and telecommunications companies.

"Amdahl's goal, simply stated, is to be our customers' trusted, indispensable vendor of enterprise computing solutions," Wright wrote in the 1998 corporate brochure. "To accomplish this, we have adopted a services-oriented, two-tiered strategy that addresses customer requirements in the areas of both applications and computing infrastructure."[19]

Wright went on to lead the company through a restructuring process, creating a business model that would support the corporate vision to design, manage and maintain large, mission-critical computing systems. In November 1999, Wright announced the formation of four operating groups to more clearly focus efforts on individual businesses. The groups included:

- Technology, emphasizing servers, storage, and packaged offerings;
- Software, whose objective is increasing intellectual property with a special focus on automated storage management and performance management;
- IT Services and Support, concentrating on infrastructure and operational services and product support; and
- Business Solutions, which consists of the DMR Consulting Group delivering application and systems development, including business intelligence and extended enterprise applications.

Each of these four business divisions is responsible for its own profitability, research and development, product-specific marketing, partner selection, and development of broadly expanded sales channels. Organizing into divisions places each person in the company in a position to focus clearly on a specific business. At the same time, the new organizational structure maintains the flexibility necessary for cooperation among the businesses, ensuring that customer solutions include the full range and optimum mix of hardware, software consulting, and services.

Overlaying the divisional structure, Wright in December 1999 announced the formation of a new Strategic Accounts Team to develop and strengthen strategic partnerships with selected accounts. Chartered to significantly increase revenues and broaden account penetration, the Strategic Accounts Team management focuses specifically on industry and executive relationships and supports the divisions with sales planning and campaigns.

Driving everything from the corporate strategy to the new business model is the clear recognition of increasing opportunities the Internet offers for customers' businesses.

"Most of our customers are enabling their enterprise applications to embrace e-business opportunities," said Wright. "This means they need support not only in designing and building their extended enterprises, but in ensuring that their technology infrastructures are effectively managed and continuously available."[20]

Amdahl is well positioned to respond to these needs. For nearly 30 years, Amdahl's historic competencies had been rooted in its ability to build, manage and maintain very large, mission-critical computing environments.

"Amdahl customers have been among the most aggressive and innovative users of information technology worldwide, and our investments in technology have been targeted toward the very complex data processing environments that support large-scale computing," Wright remarked near the end of 1998.[21] Those investments paid off as Amdahl was able to move its legacy skills of providing continuous availability, back-up recovery, data management and system integration from the traditional "back office" of operational and administrative support and "front office" of customer relationship management to the new world of the extended enterprise and e-business.

Marshalling around the theme "We Deliver," the company is focused on delivering what it calls "the RAS (reliability, availability, and scalability) in dotcom."

Amdahl's Legacy and Its Future

In the 21st century, Amdahl remains true to its roots. The company's tradition of competitiveness, flexibility and a strategy that focuses on the customer is unchanged. And, although its fortunes are no longer exclusively tied to the large mainframes, its unique strength is still its broad expertise in the largest and most complex computing environments.

The Amdahl story is an important chapter in the history of computing. As the first real challenger to IBM's monopolistic control over large-scale computing, Amdahl paved the way toward highly compatible open systems environments in which customers have several choices in their decisions about IT infrastructure. Thousands of businesses and ultimately the world's consumers benefited from the competition as prices fell, computing speed and capacity increased dramatically, service and support were enhanced, and product development cycles were shortened.

With three decades of experience and an increasingly strong partnership with Fujitsu, Wright predicts that Amdahl will break $3 billion in revenues by 2003. Most of this growth will come from the DMR Consulting Group, recognized as a premier provider of e-business solutions, and from the rapidly expanding infrastructure services organization within Amdahl. The company will also continue its collaboration with Fujitsu on a wide range of storage and server products, while shifting its focus from simply providing hardware to implementing it as part of a total solutions package.

To accomplish its long-range business objectives, Amdahl plans to use a combination of acquisitions, flexible internal growth models, emerging market opportunities and the formation of strategic partnerships. In particular, the company's alliance with Microsoft is expected to broaden the

Amdahl's headquarters, located in Sunnyvale. Since its first machine was introduced in 1975, Amdahl has transformed itself from IBM's only viable mainframe competition into a large-scale solutions provider.

penetration of Amdahl products and services in Windows NT environments.

"The reality of what we've done," said Wright, "is that we've gone back to our core competencies. We've realized what our baseline value is, and it is intellectual capital and our ability to deliver solutions and results to the customer. For the future, we will continue to adapt to changes in our dynamic marketplace, but always keeping our focus on our customers and on the traditional strengths we embrace."[22]

With a total focus on the customer, a prized reputation for delivering premier solutions and an employee population that holds a stunning depth and breadth of knowledge and industry expertise, the company promises to move smoothly through its transition to a solutions company, building on the foundation of the past to address the opportunities of the future.

Notes to Sources

Chapter One

1. Gene Amdahl, interviewed by the author, April, 25, 1996. Transcript, p. 34.
2. Fred Warshofsky, *The Chip War* (New York: Charles Scribner's Sons, 1989), p. 18.
3. Ibid., p. 20.
4. International Business Machines Corporation, *Innovation in IBM Computer Technology*, (Armonk, New York: International Business Machines, 1984), p. 4.
5. "A Brief History of IBM in San Jose," unpublished, no date.
6. *Innovation in IBM Computer Technology*, p. 3.
7. Hans Queisser, *The Conquest of the Microchip* (Cambridge, Mass.: Harvard University Press, 1989), pp. 69, 203.
8. Hanson, *Innovation in IBM Computer Technology*, p. 7.
9. Ibid., p. 6.
10. Dick Hanson, *The New Alchemists* (Boston, Massachusetts: Little, Brown and Company, 1982), p. 103.
11. Michael S. Malone, *The Big Score* (Garden City, New York: Doubleday & Company, Inc., 1985), p. 311.
12. Gene Amdahl, interviewed by author, April 25, 1996. Transcript, p. 34.
13. Gene Amdahl, interviewed by author, April 15, 1996. Transcript, p. 21.
14. Ibid., p. 26.
15. Hanson, *The New Alchemists*, p. 104.
16. Ibid.
17. "Before Amdahl Corporation," unpublished, 1979.
18. "A History of Amdahl," unpublished document, circa 1981.
19. Gene Amdahl, interviewed by the author, April 15, 1996. Transcript, p. 16.
20. Malone, *The Big Score*, p. 263.

Chapter Two

1. Lyle Topham, interviewed by the author, March 7, 1996. Transcript, p. 2.
2. Amdahl Corporation Corporate Background, 1993. p. 1.
3. Harold O. Shattuck, interviewed by the author, March 7, 1996. Transcript, p. 12.
4. Gene M. Amdahl, "The Early Chapters of the PCM Story," *Datamation*, February 1979, p. 114.
5. Scott Schmedel, "Taking On An Industry Giant," *Harvard Business Review*, March/April 1980, p. 86.
6. Amdahl, "Early Chapters," p. 115.
7. Ibid.
8. "Amdahl's Assault on the IBM 360," *Business Week*, March 10, 1973, pp. 62–63.
9. Ned Heizer, interviewed by the author, October 1, 1996. Transcript, p. 4.
10. Amdahl, "Early Chapters," p. 115.
11. "Attacking on the Flank," *Computer*, March 1973.
12. Robert Maier, interviewed by the author, March 6, 1996. Transcript, p. 2.
13. Topham, interview, p. 2.
14. Joe Francesconi, interviewed by the author, September 24, 1996. Transcript, p. 8.
15. Dave Brewer, interviewed by the author, March 8, 1996. Transcript, p. 8.
16. Amdahl interview, p. 40.

17. P. Franson, "Amdahl Proved You Could Compete With IBM," *Electronic Business*, March 1979.
18. Larsen interview, p. 5.
19. Bill Flanagan, interviewed by the author, April 15, 1996. Transcript, p. 4.
20. Henry Cassel, interviewed by the author, March 6, 1996. Transcript, p. 8.
21. International Business Machines Corporation, *Innovation in IBM Computer Technology*, Armonk, NY.
22. Warshofsky, *Chip War*, pp. 121–122.
23. Brewer interview, p. 32.
24. Amdahl interview, April 15, 1996.
25. Bert O'Neill, interviewed by the author, September 23, 1996. Transcript, p. 18.
26. Amdahl — Annual Status Report — 1974, p. 12.
27. Dave Brewer and Bruce Beebe, interviewed by Jeffrey Rodengen, March 6, 1996, pp. 35–36.
28. Yoshiro Yoshioka, interviewed by the author, April 15, 1996. Transcript, p. 5.
29. Amdahl, "Early Chapters," p. 115.
30. Ibid.
31. 1976 Annual Report, Amdahl Corporation, Sunnyvale, CA, p. 20.
32. Larsen interview, p. 8.
33. Hesh Wiener, "Outdoing IBM: The Amdahl Challenge," *Computer Decisions*, March 3, 1973, p. 19.
34. Scott Schmedel, "Taking On an Industry Giant," p. 87.
35. "Attacking on the Flank," *Computer*, March 1973, p. 39.
36. Mary Jo Ignoffo, *Sunnyvale: From the City of Destiny to the Heart of Silicon Valley*, Cupertino, CA: California History Center Foundation, 1994, pp. 78, 79–80.
37. Gene M. Amdahl, "Early Chapters," p. 115.
38. Daniel Yankelovich, Inc., *A Study of Market Opportunity and Potential for a Large Computer System (Among Large Computer Users)* Prepared for Amdahl Corporation, July 1973, pp. 8, 14, 33, 63, 72, 74, 81.
39. International Data Corporation, *IBM Medium-Scale Computer Market*, July 1973, D-6.
40. Scott Schmedel, "Taking On an Industry Giant," p. 87.
41. Topham interview, p. 4.
42. Shattuck interview, pp. 17–18.
43. Ed Cardinal, interviewed by the author, March 6, 1996. Transcript, p. 3.
44. Beebe interview, p. 19.
45. Amdahl, "Early Chapters," pp. 115–116.
46. Brewer and Beebe interview, p. 16.
47. Robert Maier, interviewed by the author, March 6, 1996. Transcript, p. 16.
48. Position Statement, March 18, 1974 (Amdahl Employees).
49. Anderson interview, p. 9.
50. Brewer and Beebe interview, p. 38.
51. Gene White, interviewed by the author, September 20, 1996. Transcript, p. 7.
52. "A Tyro Challenges IBM in Big Computers," *Business Week*, May 12, 1975, p. 67.
53. White interview, p. 2.
54. Ibid., pp. 4–5.
55. 1976 Annual Report, Amdahl Corporation, Sunnyvale, CA, p. 20.
56. Anderson interview, p. 12.
57. Amdahl, "Early Chapters," p. 116.

58. News Release, September 11, 1974, Amdahl Corporation, Sunnyvale, CA.
59. Amdahl, "Early Chapters," p. 116.
60. Amdahl — Annual Status Report — 1974, pp. 1, 2, 8, 14, 23.

Chapter Three

1. James K. Dutton, interviewed by the author, March 6, 1996. Transcript, p. 19.
2. News Release, October 24, 1975, Amdahl Corporation, Sunnyvale, CA; "Use of ECL LSI in Amdahl Computer Clips IBM's Wings," *Electronic Engineering Times*, November 3, 1975.
3. "Has Amdahl Got A Billion Dollar Baby?" *Computer Decisions*, April, 1975, p. 2.
4. Ray Williams, interviewed with Gene Amdahl, by the author, April 15, 1996. Transcript, p. 53.
5. Bro Uttal, "Gene Amdahl Takes Aim at IBM," *Fortune*, 1977.
6. Ken Simonds, interviewed by the author, September 25, 1996. Transcript, p. 5.
7. White interviewed, p. 5.
8. Joan A. Tharp, "Amdahl Corp.'s Eugene R. White," *The Executive SF*, August 1981, p. 6.
9. Charlie Pratt, interviewed by author, March 7, 1996. Transcript, pp. 8–9.
10. "A Tyro Challenges IBM," p. 67.
11. "Early Customers Gamble on an Upstart," *Amdahl Update*, June 1985, p. 9.
12. Ibid.
13. "A Tyro Challenges IBM," p. 67.
14. John Matthews, interviewed by the author, March 6, 1996. Transcript, pp. 11–12.
15. Schmedel, "Taking On an Industry Giant," p. 90.
16. Flanagan interviewed, pp. 6–7.
17. News Release, October 24, 1975.
18. Amdahl, "Early Chapters."
19. Dutton interview, pp. 16, 19.
20. Francesconi interview, p. 9.
21. News Release, October 24, 1975.
22. "Tales from the Field," *Amdahl Update*, June 1985, p. 12.
23. Pratt interview, p. 7.
24. "Tales from the Field," p. 12.
25. Don Leavitt, "Michigan Accepts Amdahl 470 After Tests," *Computerworld*, October 15, 1975, p. 5.
26. Ibid., p. 4.
27. "Early Customers," p. 9.
28. News Release, October 24, 1975, p. 6.
29. "Tales from the Field," p. 12.
30. Amdahl interview, April 15, 1996, pp. 45–46.
31. "Sales History From Inception Through December 1977," unpublished document, Amdahl Corporation Archives, Sunnyvale, CA, p. 1.
32. Dutton interview, p. 17.
33. "Early Customers," pp. 9–10.
34. Uttal, "Gene Amdahl Takes Aim."
35. "Early Customers," p. 10.
36. 1976 Annual Report, Amdahl Corporation, Sunnyvale, CA, 1977, pp. 20–21.

Chapter Four

1. "The Beginning and Continuing of Pride," *Amdahl Update*, November 1990, p. 11.

2. "Eastward Ho!" *Amdahl Update*, November 1990, p. 14.
3. Peter Williams, interviewed by the author, October 25, 1996. Transcript, p. 5.
4. Ray Williams, interview, p. 55.
5. William F. Ferone, interviewed by the author, April 15, 1996. Transcript, p. 4.
6. Matthews, interview, p. 8.
7. Uttal, "Gene Amdahl Takes Aim."
8. Cassel interview, p. 24.
9. Fred Gonzalez, interviewed by the author, September 23, 1996. Transcript, p. 3.
10. Ollie J. Nutt, interviewed by the author, September 24, 1996. Transcript, p. 8.
11. Wayne McIntyre, interviewed by the author, March 6, 1996. Transcript, p. 4.
12. "Sales History," p. 1.
13. 1976 Annual Report, Amdahl Corporation, Sunnyvale, CA, p. 12.
14. Cardinal interview, p. 7.
15. "Sales History," p. 1.
16. Cardinal interview, p. 7.
17. Gene Amdahl interview, p. 61.
18. McIntyre interview, p. 16.
19. Ed Thompson, interviewed by the author, April 16, 1996. Transcript, pp. 10, 12.
20. 1976 Annual Report, p. 2.
21. Gene Plonka, interviewed by the author, September 23, 1996. Transcript, p. 2.
22. White interview, p. 6.
23. 1976 Annual Report, p. 9.
24. 1976 Annual Report, p. 11.
25. Steve Coggins, interviewed by the author, September 23, 1996. Transcript, p. 6.
26. Uttal, "Gene Amdahl Takes Aim."
27. Securities and Exchange Commission, Form 10-K, Amdahl Corporation, Sunnyvale, CA, December 30, 1977, p. 8.
28. Alan Bell, interviewed by the author, October 15, 1996. Transcript, p. 12.
29. Tharp, "Amdahl Corp.'s Eugene R. White," p. 6.
30. Uttal, "Gene Amdahl Takes Aim."
31. Peter Williams interview, p. 13.
32. 1976 Annual Report, p. 20.
33. 1976 Annual Report, p. 11.
34. O'Neill interview, p. 7.
35. Uttal, "Gene Amdahl Takes Aim."
36. News Release, March 28, 1977, Amdahl Corporation, Sunnyvale, CA.
37. Ibid.
38. Ibid.
39. "Michelson/Morley Award to Amdahl," *Amdahl Times*, June 1977, p. 2.
40. John Foggiato, "Integrated Circuit Facility," *Amdahl Times*, June 1977, p. 3.
41. Jack Lewis, interviewed by the author, June 17, 1995. Transcript, p. 4.
42. Ibid., p. 2.
43. Ibid., p. 3.
44. Ibid., pp. 4–5.
45. Tony Pozos, interviewed by the author, April 15, 1996. Transcript, pp. 6–7.
46. Uttal, "Amdahl Takes Aim."
47. "Ireland Plant Opens," *Amdahl Update*, July/August 1978, p. 5.
48. "Spreading the Good News," p. 46.
49. Dick Sayford, "A Telex From Europe — With Love!?!" *Amdahl Times*, June 1977, p. 3.
50. Form 10-K, pp. 5–6.
51. Lewis interview, p. 7.
52. Uttal, "Amdahl Takes Aim."

Chapter Five

1. "Amdahl History Slide Presentation," transcript, Eugene R. White, Clifford J.

Madden, John Lewis, Gene Amdahl, (unpublished), spring 1978.
2. Mullally, John J., "Amdahl No David to IBM's Goliath," *Industry Week*, Oct. 2, 1978, p. 4.
3. Ed Thompson interview, p. 4.
4. Ernest B. Thompson, interviewed by the author, April 16, 1996. Transcript, p. 6.
5. 1978 Annual Report, Amdahl Corporation, Sunnyvale, CA, pp. 9, 11, 19.
6. "Rapid Growth Reflected in Expanding Facilities," Amdahl Update, First Quarter, 1979, p. 5.
7. Ibid.
8. "Building on Success," *Amdahl Update*, June 1985, p. 15.
9. News Release, June 4, 1979, Amdahl Corporation, Sunnyvale, CA.
10. News Release, September 1979, Amdahl Corporation, Sunnyvale, CA.
11. "Round the World With Amdahl," *Amdahl Update*, Second Quarter 1979, p. 9.
12. "Facilities/Staff Continue to Expand," *Amdahl Update*, July/August 1978, p. 1.
13. Pozos interview, p. 2.
14. Flanagan interview, pp. 10–11.
15. 1979 Annual Report, p. 8.
16. "New Products Introduced by Amdahl," *Amdahl Update*, Third Quarter 1979, p. 10.
17. Gene White, interviewed by Tony Spaeth or *Forbes* magazine, November 20, 1978, pp. 1–2.
18. Dave Chambers, interviewed by Karen Nitkin, July 23, 1996. Transcript, p. 2.
19. Mullally, "Amdahl No David," p. 40.
20. "Amdahl Women's Network," *Amdahl Update*, Supplement V 1, No. 2, September 1979, p. 3.
21. Mark N. Dodosh, Kathryn Christensen, "Amdahl's Founder Resigns as Consultant to Form Competing Computer Company," *Wall Street Journal*, August 18, 1980.
22. Schmedel, "Taking On An Industry Giant," p. 92.
23. Memo from J.C. Lewis to all employees, dated August 2, 1979.
24. "Memorex Corporation," Number Nine in the Datamation 100, *Datamation*, July 1980.
25. "Amdahl, STC Plan Merger, New Firm," *Electronic News*, April 7, 1980, p. 14.
26. Tom Cullen, "2 Factors Seen Killing Amdahl/STC Tie," *Electronic Engineering Times*, July 7, 1980, pp. 1–2.
27. "Amdahl Agrees to Acquire Tran. Tel for About $26 Million," *Electronic News*, March 24, 1980.
28. Securities and Exchange Commission, Form 10-K, Amdahl Corporation, Sunnyvale, CA, December 26, 1980, p. 1.
29. 1980 Annual Report, Amdahl Corporation, Sunnyvale, CA, p. 3.
30. 1980 Annual Report, Amdahl Corporation, Sunnyvale, CA, p. 19.
31. E. Drake Lundell, Jr., "Amdahl, Nasco Tops in IBM's Own Ratings," *Computerworld*, July 14, 1980, pp. 1–2.
32. 1980 Annual Report, p. 3.
33. 1980 Annual Report, p. 3.
34. "New Products," p. 10.
35. Ibid.
36. Gene White, interviewed by Tony Spaeth for *Forbes* magazine, November 20, 1978. Transcript, p. 4.
37. DeMory interview, p. 10.

Chapter Six

1. DeMory interview, p. 10.

2. Gary Putka, "Amdahl Price Cuts on New Line didn't Surprise Analysts Who Cite Stiffer Competition by IBM," *Wall Street Journal*, October 1982.
3. Tharp, "Amdahl Corp.'s Eugene R. White," p. 7.
4. Michael Kolbenschlag, "The Best of Friends," *Forbes*, December 8, 1980, p. 40.
5. 1980 Annual Report, p. 2.
6. Ibid., p. 8.
7. Ibid., pp. 8–9.
8. *Electronic Packaging and Production*, January 1981, pp. 70–71.
9. Brewer interview, p. 48.
10. Cassel interview, p. 26.
11. Allen Buskirk, interviewed by the author, March 7, 1996. Transcript, p. 23.
12. Lewis interview, p. 31.
13. News Release, October 27, 1981, Amdahl Corporation, Sunnyvale, CA.
14. *UTS Systems, Large-Scale File Serving Solutions*, Amdahl Corporation brochure, November 1989.
15. Amdahl UTS backgrounder, no date.
16. "Today's Ledger," *Peninsula Times Tribune*, November 14, 1984.
17. Edward K. Yasaki, "Amdahl vs. The World," *Datamation*, August, 1983, p. 81.
18. Gill, Philip J., "Amdahl Execs Say 580 Will Be Mainstay Product," *Information Systems News*, November 29, 1982.
19. "Can Amdahl Take the Heat?" *Financial World*, October 15, 1982, p. 49.
20. "Amdahl Arranges $370 Million Credit," *Wall Street Journal*, October 20, 1981; 1981 Annual Report, pp. 2–3.
21. News Release, January 29, 1982, Amdahl Corporation, Sunnyvale, CA.
22. News Release, February 16, 1982, Amdahl Corporation, Sunnyvale, CA.
23. John Adler, interviewed by the author, September 24, 1996.
24. "Can Amdahl Take the Heat?" p. 48.
25. Ibid.
26. Adler interview.
27. DeMory interview, p. 10.
28. Dave Chambers, interviewed by Karen Nitkin, July 23, 1996. Transcript, p. 8.
29. Dave Brewer, letter to Bill Stewart, December 10, 1997.
30. DeMory interview, p. 11.
31. Dave Brewer, interviewed by Karen Nitkin, July 23, 1996. Transcript, p. 6.
32. Matthew interview, p. 22.
33. Ferone interview, p. 21.
34. Matthews interview, p. 21.
35. News Release, September 30, 1996, Amdahl Corporation, Sunnyvale, CA.
36. Gill, "Amdahl Execs Say 580," p. 6.
37. Paul E. Schindler, Jr., "Amdahl Already Running IBM's MVS/XA On Its 470," *Information Systems News*, October 31, 1983.
38. 1982 Annual Report, Amdahl Corporation, Sunnyvale, CA, pp. 1–3.
39. Michael B. Shahbazian, interviewed by the author, September 23, 1996. Transcript, p. 7.
40. Evelyn Richards, "Amdahl Pins Hopes On Latest Computer," *San Jose Mercury News*, 1982.
41. News Release, May 27, 1982, Amdahl Corporation, Sunnyvale, CA.
42. Gill, "Amdahl Execs say 580," p. 6.
43. "6000 Series Selling Well," *Amdahl Update*, May 1983, p. 2.
44. "Amdahl Corporation," Hambrecht & Quist Incorporated, (Unpublished document), April, 1983, p. 47.

45. "Ireland Builds First 580," *Amdahl Update*, May, 1983, p. 2.
46. Bagamery, Anne, "No risk, no reward," *Forbes*, September 26, 1983, p. 98.
47. Ibid.
48. "4705E: A Faster Front-End Processor," *Amdahl Update*, May 1983, p. 3.
49. "Amdahl a Fortune 500 Company," *Amdahl Update*, May 1983, p. 3.
50. "Amdahl Names Lewis To Added Post of Chief," *Wall Street Journal*, May 18, 1983.
51. Thompson interview, p. 31.
52. Memorandum, from Wendy Matthews — Manager Corporate Communications To Dave McGlaughlin, March 18, 1983.
53. "A Letter from the President," Amdahl Update, May 1983, p. 1.
54. Cassel interview, pp. 20–21.
55. News Release, June 3, 1983, Amdahl Corporation, Sunnyvale, CA.
56 "Amdahl, Wang, Sperry Win Big Contracts," *EDP Industry News*, June 20, 1983, p. 8.
57. Norman Kemp, "Men At Work," *Datamation*, August, 1983, p. 84.
58. 1983 Annual Report, Amdahl Corporation, Sunnyvale, CA, pp. 3, 39.
59. "Marketing News," June 13, 1983, Unpublished document, Amdahl Corporation, Sunnyvale, CA, pp. 4–5.
60. Ibid., pp. 1–2.
61. "Why Only Japan Has The Muscle to Copy IBM," *Business Week*, May 28, 1984, p. 103.
62. "Amdahl Announces MVS/XA Support And New 580 Series Extensions," *Europa Report*, July 25, 1983.
63. Paul Gillin, "Firm to Support Four IMS Copies On Lone CPU using MVS/XA," *Computerworld*, July 30, 1984, p. 9.
64. Paul E. Schindler, Jr., "Amdahl Reports 5-Month Large-Drive Backlog," *Information Systems News*, August 6, 1984, p. 29.
65. 1983 Annual Report, Amdahl Corporation, Sunnyvale, CA, p. 1.
66. "Amdahl Cuts Computer Prices, Announces Two New Models," *San Jose Mercury News*, March 2, 1984.
67. News Release, March 1, 1984, Amdahl Corporation, Sunnyvale, CA.
68. News Release, January 18, 1984, Amdahl Corporation, Sunnyvale, CA.
69. David Zielenziger, "Amdahl Chief Pleads For More Time From Wall Street," *Electronic Engineering Times*, April 8, 1984, p. 36.
70. "Rating Computer Companies: And the Winner Is ...," *Business Week*, July 30, 1984, p. 110.
71. Heizer, p. 7.
72. Mary A.C. Fallon, "Staying Power," *San Jose Mercury News*, August 20, 1984, p. 3.
73. Gene White, interviewed by the author, September 20, 1996. Transcript, p. 14.
74. Bert O, Neill, interviewed by the author, September 23, 1996. Transcript, p. 15.
75. News Release, August 15, 1984, Amdahl Corporation, Sunnyvale, CA.
76. Paul E. Schindler, Jr., "Amdahl Reports 5-Month Large-Drive Backlog," Information Systems News, August 6, 1983, p. 28.
77. Greg Handschuh, interviewed by the author, September 23, 1996. Transcript, p. 13.
78. "Why Only Japan," pp. 102–103.
79. Fallon, "Staying Power," p. 20.
80. "Japanese Jitters ...," *The IBM System User*, May, 1984, p. 21.
81. Michael Tyler, "Amdahl's Super CPU Gamble," *Datamation*, November 1, 1984, p. 38.

82. 1984 Annual Report, Amdahl Corporation, Sunnyvale, CA, p. 2.
83. "R&D Scoreboard," *Business Week*, July 8, 1985, p. 94.
84. 1984 Amdahl Annual Report, p. 5.

Chapter Seven

1. Paul E. Schindler, Jr., "Amdahl Releases High-MIPS Apache," *InformationWEEK*, October 28, 1985, p. 14.
2. "Amdahl Names New Senior Exec," *San Jose Mercury News*, April 10, 1985.
3. Joe Zemke, interviewed by the author, June 17, 1996. Transcript, pp. 7–8.
4. Paul E. Schindler, Jr., "Amdahl's Growth Triggers Shift," *InformationWEEK*, April 25, 1985, p. 25.
5. Jeff Moad, "Amdahl Taps Opns. Chief; Restructure," *Electronic News*, April 15, 1985, p. 21.
6. Brewer and Beebe interview, pp 1–2.
7. Robert Buday, "Airline Service Bureau May Bump Amdahl For IBM," *InformationWEEK*, July 15, 1985, p. 38.
8. News Release, January 21, 1985, Amdahl Corporation, Sunnyvale, CA.
9. Shahbazian interview, p. 9.
10. "Company Notes," *Europa Report*, July 16, 1985, p. 8.
11. Chambers interviewed, pp. 9–10.
12. Buskirk interview, p. 24.
13. Zemke interview, p. 36.
14. Paul E. Schindler, Jr., "Amdahl Releases High-MIPS Apache," *InformationWEEK*, October 28, 1985, p. 13.
15. Paul E. Schindler, Jr., "Southland Lands First Amdahl 5890," *InformationWEEK*, August 11, 1986, p. 14.
16. Jeffrey Beeler, "Amdahl Learns Its Lessons," *Computerworld*, September 8, 1986, p. 41.
17. "Amdahl Goes In," *Computer Weekly*, April 9, 1987.
18. "Amdahl Exec: Things Don't Get Much Better Than This'," *CMS Bulletin*, August 29, 1986.
19. News Release, August 6, 1986, Amdahl Corporation, Sunnyvale, CA.
20. Michael W. Miller, "Amdahl Will Unveil A Mainframe Line Designed To Compete With IBM Family," *Wall Street Journal*, October 22, 1985, p. 16.
21. Paul E. Schindler, Jr., "Amdahl Releases High-MIPS Apache," *InformationWEEK*, October 28, 1985.
22. Eric Nee, "Amdahl Exec: IBM Pricing to Cool Down," *Computer News*, September 1, 1986, p. 19.
23. John W. Wilson, Barbara Beull, "Who's Afraid of Big Blue? Not These Two." *Business Week*, October 6, 1986, p. 86.
24. News Release, January 16, 1986, Amdahl Corporation, Sunnyvale, CA.
25. News Release, April 22, 1986, Amdahl Corporation, Sunnyvale, CA; Paul E. Shindler, Jr., "Amdahl Disk Drives Now In A Solid State," *InformationWEEK*, April 28, 1986, p. 22.
26. Jeffrey Beeler, "Amdahl Adds Storage Module To Disk Line, Improves Terminal Response Time Tenfold," *Computerworld*, April 28, 1986, p. 10.
27. James Connolly, "Amdahl Hikes High-End Disk Drive Capacity," *Computerworld*, December 9, 1985.
28. Jeffrey Beeler, "Amdahl Broadens Unix-Based UTS Line," *Computerworld*, January 26, 1986, p. 13.

29. Steve Polilli, "Amdahl Aspen Viability Meets with Skepticism," *MISWeek*, January 13, 1986.
30. Kathy Chin Leong, "Amdahl Kills Aspen Plan, Favors Unix," *Computerworld*, November 2, 1987, pp. 1, 10.
31. James Fallon, "Amdahl Opens $15M European HQ in Britain," *Management Information Systems Week*, June 23, 1986, p. 12.
32. Bell interview, p. 4.
33. 1986 Annual Report, Amdahl Corporation, Sunnyvale, CA, p. 2.
34. "Amdahl Predicts a Billion-Dollar Year," *InformationWEEK*, July 13, 1987, p. 23.
35. 1986 Annual Report, p. 6.

Chapter Eight

1. Marc Beauchamp, "Learning From Disaster," *Forbes*, October 19, 1987, p. 96.
2. Lewis interview, p. 18.
3. Paul E. Schindler, Jr., "NAS, Amdahl Are Most Reliable," *InformationWEEK*, July 6, 1987, p. 11.
4. "Amdahl Predicts A Billion-Dollar Year," p. 22.
5. David William, "Some High-Tech Firms See Harm In Tariffs," *San Jose Mercury News*, April 14, 1987, pp. 1, 14A.
6. Ray Alvarestorres, "Lewis Named Amdahl Corp. Chairman," *San Jose Mercury News*, May 29, 1987, p. 17F.
7. News Release, June 9, 1987, Amdahl Corporation, Sunnyvale, CA.
8. News Release, September 15, 1987, Amdahl Corporation, Sunnyvale, CA.
9. Charlie Bruno, "Amdahl Bills New Processors As 80% Faster Than Old Models," *Communications Week*, September 21, 1987, p. 17.
10. News Release, May 16, 1988, Amdahl Corporation, Sunnyvale, CA.
11. Lewis interview, p. 31.
12. News Release, August 28, 1989, Amdahl Corporation, Sunnyvale, CA.
13. 1987 Annual Report, Amdahl Corporation, Sunnyvale, CA, p. 1.
14. Anne Knowles, "Can Amdahl Always Follow Big Blue's Zig-Zags?" *Electronic Business*, November 1, 1988, pp. 58–61.
15. Bro Uttal, "Companies that Serve You Best," *Fortune*, December 7, 1987.
16. "The Silicon Valley 100," *San Jose Mercury News*, May 23, 1987, p. D-1.
17. News Release, February 9, 1988, Amdahl Corporation, Sunnyvale, CA.
18. Virginia Dudek, "High, Low-End Unix Alliances Merge," *Management Information Systems Week*, February 15, 1988, p. 1.
19. J.A. Savage, "Amdahl Topped IBM MIPS," *Computerworld*, May 9, 1988, p. 1.
20. Knowles, "Can Amdahl Always Follow Big Blue's Zig-Zags," p. 58.
21. James P. Miller, "Amdahl Unveils A Faster Line of Computers," *Wall Street Journal*, May 4, 1988, p. 4.
22. News Release, May 3, 1988, Amdahl Corporation, Sunnyvale, CA.
23. Paul E. Schindler, Jr., and Lisa Stapleton, "Amdahl Leapfrogs," *InformationWEEK*, May 9, 1988, p. 11.
24. Cassel interview, p. 29.
25. 1988 Annual Report, Amdahl Corporation, p. 8.
26. Mary Kathleen Flynn, "Amdahl 5990 Series Boasts 50 percent Performance Gain," *Datamation*, July 1, 1988, p. 79.

27. News Release, June 27, 1996, Amdahl Corporation, Sunnyvale, CA.
28. 1988 Annual Report, Amdahl Corporation, Sunnyvale, CA, p. 1.
29. Michael Fibs, "Big Blue's 'Cold' Chills Chip Firms," *San Jose Mercury News*, October 24, 1988.
30. "Corporate Critics Confidential," *Wall Street Journal*, October 24, 1988.
31. Mark Lapedus, "Hear Amdahl Ends SuperCPU Effort," *Electronic News*, September 10, 1990. Corporation, Sunnyvale, CA, p. 9.
32. J.A. Savage, "Three Amdahl Models Invigorate 5990 Series," *Computerworld*, May 1, 1989.
33. Mary Anne Ostrom, "Amdahl Buys Four Buildings in North San Jose From Mozart," *San Jose Mercury News*, April 27, 1989, p. 8F.
34. "World's Largest Prime Number Has Been Calculated; Now What?" *San Jose Mercury News*, August 30, 1989, p. C-1; Barry A. Cipra, "Math Teams Vaults Over Prime Record," *Science*, August 25, 1989, p. 815.
35. 1989 Annual Report, Amdahl Corporation, Sunnyvale, CA, pp. 19–20.
36. Lee Gomes, "400 Laid Off At Amdahl," *San Jose Mercury News*, pp. 10F, 14F.
37. Steve Kaufman, "Amdahl Firing Forgets People," *San Jose Mercury News*, December 4, 1989, p. 1D.
38. 1989 Annual Report, p. 1.

Chapter Nine

1. Jean S. Bozman, "Amdahl Taps Zemke To Get Back on Track," *Computerworld*, May 18, 1992, p. 141.
2. Lee Gomes, "Fujitsu's Chance To Buy Amdahl Nears," *San Jose Mercury News*, February 1, 1990, p. 1D.
3. Lee Gomes, "Fujitsu Denies Rumors," *San Jose Mercury News*, February 6, 1990, p 1D.
4. "Amdahl Names Unix Guru," *InformationWEEK*, May 14, 1990, p. 15.
5. Mark Lapedus, "Amdahl Taps Exec for Unix Effort," *Electronic News*, May 7, 1990, p. 12.
6. Mark Lapedus, "Hear Amdahl Ends SuperCPU Effort," p. 8.
7. News Release, November 7, 1989, Amdahl Corporation, Sunnyvale, CA.
8. Lapedus, "Amdahl Taps Exec," p. 12.
9. Susan C. Faludi, "Amdahl Plans Most Powerful Mainframes Yet," *Wall Street Journal*, September 19, 1990, p. B4.
10. Ron Wolf," Amdahl Tops In Computer Speed," *San Jose Mercury News*, September 19, 1990, p. 70.
11. Jean S. Bozman, "Growth Path in Key For 5995M Buyer," *Computerworld*, August 17, 1992, p. 61.
12. 1990 Annual Report, Amdahl Corporation, Sunnyvale, CA, pp. 1–4.
13. Jean S. Bozman, "Amdahl Selects Sparc For Unix Server/Hosts," *Computerworld*, February 18, 1991, p. 8.
14. News Release, December 11, 1990, Amdahl Corporation, Sunnyvale, CA.
15. Ed Sperling, "Amdahl Bolsters Unix Line," Computer Systems News, October 8, 1990, p. 29; Jean S. Bozman, "Amdahl Whips Latest Release Into Unix Shape," *Computerworld*, October 15, 1990, p. 34.
16. Bozman, "Amdahl Whips Latest Release," p. 34.
17. S.A. Maud, "Amdahl OS Will Comply With GOSIP," *Government Computer News*, June 10, 1991, pp. 1, 89.

18. News Release, March 26, 1991, Amdahl Corporation, Sunnyvale, CA.
19. Helge Knudsen, interviewed by Karen Nitkin, July 12, 1996. Transcript, p. 17.
20. Jean S. Bozman, "Amdahl Takes A Look At Pricing To Increase Sales," *Computerworld*, May 20, 1991, p. 118; Rosemary Hamilton, "Amdahl Eyes AD/Cycle Turf," *Computerworld*, March 25, 1991, p. 1; Sarah Aryanpur, "Amdahl Offers Users An AD/Cycle Alternative," *Computer Weekly*, April 4, 1991, p. 1; Andre Fuochi, "Canada's Mr. Huron' Leads Amdahl Development Effort," *Computing Canada*, May 9, 1991, pp. 1–4.
21. Katy Ring, "Objects Clog Up the Cycle," *IBM System User*, June 1992, p. 25.
22. Knudsen interview, p. 29.
23. News Release, May 28, 1992, Amdahl Corporation, Sunnyvale, CA.
24. "Amdahl Profits Plunge 86%," *San Jose Mercury News*, July 27, 1991, p. 1F.
25. Cassel interview, pp. 37–38.
26. Mark Lapedus, "Amdahl CPU Chief To Run Storage Unit," *Electronic News*, August 26, 1991, pp. 11–12; P. Morgan Shepard, "Amdahl's Newest Processor Helps Availability," *Service News*, November, 1991, p. 10; Michail L. Sullivan-Trainor, "Amdahl, Hitachi Tie For Top User Ratings," *Computerworld*, August 19, 1991, p. 56.
27. Jean S. Bozman, "Amdahl Alerts Customers To Defective Disk Drives," *Computerworld*, November 18, 1991, pp. 1, 117.
28. "Amdahl 6390 Delivery Set," *Computerworld*, January 20, 1991, p. 11.
29. Emma Haughton, "Viglen and Amdahl Top Supplier Quality League," *Computer Weekly*, September 5, 1991, p. 5.
30. "Industry Almanac," *Computerworld*, November 4, 1991, p. 117; Jean S. Bozman, "Amdahl Big-Iron Deliveries Slow," *Computerworld*, November 11, 1191, p. 10.
31. Jean S. Bozman, "Mainframe Maker Hits Back," *Computerworld*, September 23, 1991, p. 10.
32. 1991 Annual Report, Amdahl Corporation, Sunnyvale, CA, p. 1.
33. Tom Schlitz, "Amdahl Earnings Drop Again; Slow European Sales Blamed Again," *San Jose Mercury News*, October 23, 1991, p. 8D.
34. Jeff Moad, "The Datamation 100 — Amdahl Corp.," *Datamation*, June 15, 1992, p. 67.
35. Bozman, "Amdahl Taps Zemke," p. 141.
36. "Amdahl Offers 6390 DASD Module," *Electronic News*, January 20, 1992, p. 18.
37. "Fujitsu Raises Stake in Amdahl to 44.76 percent," *Wall Street Journal*, February 22, 1992, p. B5.
38. Zemke interview, pp. 10–12.
39. "Amdahl President Zemke is Named Chief Executive," *San Jose Mercury News*, May 8, 1992, p. 1G.
40. Gene White, interviewed by the author, September 20, 1996. Transcript, p. 19.
41. 1992 Annual Report, Amdahl Corporation, Sunnyvale, CA, p. 1.
42. Ernest B. Thompson interview, pp. 18–19.
43. Rory J. O'Connor, "Amdahl To Cut 900 Jobs," *San Jose Mercury News*, October 13, 1992, p. 1E; Steve Kaufman, "In Defense of the Mainframe," *San Jose Mercury News*, January 25, 1993, p. 7D.
44. "Company to Layoff 900, Take Third-Quarter Charge," *Wall Street Journal*, October 13,

1992; 1992 Annual Report, Amdahl Corporation, Sunnyvale, CA, p. 1.

Chapter Ten

1. Linda Alepin, interviewed by the author, April 16, 1996. Transcript, p. 21.
2. Lewis interview, p. 14.
3. Alepin interview, p. 21.
4. Lee Gomes, "Amdahl To Cut 13% of Workers," *San Jose Mercury News*, April 1993, p. 1C.
5. Shahbazian interview, p. 18.
6. John Cavalier, interviewed by the author, July 16, 1996. Transcript, p. 10.
7. Cavalier interview, p. 8.
8. News Release, August 26, 1993; 1993 Annual Report, p. 5.
9. "Enterprise-Wide Open Systems Computing: A New Evolutionary Step," published by Amdahl Corporation, Sunnyvale, CA, 1991.
10. News Release, September 21, 1993.
11. Steve Kaufman, "Amdahl-Sun Deal Is Likely to Benefit Both," *San Jose Mercury News*, September 27, 1993.
12. David B. Wright, interviewed by the author, September 24, 1996. Transcript, p. 31.
13. Wright interview, pp. 3–4.
14. Jean S. Bozman, "Amdahl Users Eye Open Systems Strategy," *Computerworld*, December 6, 1993, p. 67.
15. Zemke interview, p. 23.
16. "Fujitsu Will Help Amdahl Restructure," *San Jose Mercury News*, January, 1994.
17. Lewis interview, p. 38.
18. Topham interview, pp. 18–19.
19. DeMory interview, p. 25.
20. 1994 Annual Report, Amdahl Corporation, Sunnyvale, CA, p. 7.
21. 1994 Annual Report, Amdahl Corporation, Sunnyvale, CA, p. 7.
22. Steve Kaufman, "Amdahl Appears Well Positioned For Transition," *San Jose Mercury News*, May, 1994.
23. Lee Gomes, "For Amdahl, Mainframes Are On An Upswing," *San Jose Mercury News*, July 27, 1996, p. 7D.
24. Nutt interview, p. 22.
25. Peter Labé, interviewed by the author, October 8, 1996. Transcript, p. 14.
26. Robert D. Hof, "Amdahl Escapes 'Death Valley,' But Now What?" *Business Week*, May 16, 1994, p. 88.
27. 1994 Annual Report, p. 1.
28. Thomas Petzinger, Jr., "A Tale of Two Chips: Amdahl Decides Its Better To Be Cool," *Wall Street Journal*, August 18, 1995, p. B1.
29. News Release, February 2, 1995.
30. Amdahl "Innovation" promotional brochure for United States Fidelity and Guaranty, 1997, p. 3.
31. News Release, September 5, 1995.
32. 1995 Annual Report, p. 4.
33. 1995 Annual Report, p. 5.
34. 1995 Annual Report, pp. 4–5.

Chapter Eleven

1. Bell interview, p. 8.
2. Transcript, Michael J. Poehner, interviewed by the author, July 19, 1996, p. 7.
3. Ibid., pp. 4–5.
4. Ibid., p. 8.
5. "Who Is DMR?" *Amdahl Update*, November 16, 1995, p. 2.
6. Pierre Ducros, interviewed by the author, October 31, 1996. Transcript, p. 14.
7. Jacques Pigeon, interviewed by Kenneth D. Hartsoe, March 26, 1997. Transcript, p. 7;

"Mike Poehner Answers Questions About DMR and BSG," *Amdahl Update*, November 16, 1995, p. 3.

8. Poehner, pp. 8–9.

9. Ibid.

10. Ducros interview.

11. News Release, September 14, 1995, Amdahl Corporation, Sunnyvale, CA.

12. Poehner interview, pp. 8, 10; "Who Is DMR?" p. 1.

13. Ibid., p. 9.

14. Kim Lockhart, "DMR Tug o' War," *Canadian Lawyer*, February 1996.

15. News Release, September 14, 1995, Amdahl Corporation, Sunnyvale, CA.

16. Poehner interview, p. 11.

17. Ibid.

18. Ibid., p. 10; Lockhart, "DMR Tug o' War;" "DMR Group Acquisition Nears Completion," *GIS World*, January 1996.

19. Poehner interview, p. 12.

20. Lockhart, "DMR Tug o' War;" ; "DMR Group Acquisition Nears Completion."

21. Pigeon interview, p. 10.

22. Ibid., pp. 7, 9.

23. Poehner interview, p. 11.

24. Ibid., pp. 12–15; Lockhart, "DMR Tug o' War;" "DMR Group Acquisition Nears Completion."

25. Price Pritchett, interviewed by Kenneth D. Hartsoe, June 13, 1997. Transcript, p. 5.

26. Ibid., pp. 4, 19.

27. Ducros interview, p. 15; Pritchett interview, p. 16.

28. Pritchett interview, p. 8.

29. Pigeon interview, pp. 11–12; "Former DMR Group Managers Launch New Consulting Firm," *Dow Jones News Service*, January 24, 1996.

30. Lawrence M. Fisher, "Amdahl Chief Executive Resigns; Predecessor Will Succeed Him," *New York Times*, March 16, 1996.

31. Frank Casagrande, interviewed by Ken Hartsoe, August 20, 1997. Transcript, p. 3.

32. "Amdahl To Buy Trecom For $145Mil," Reuters America, Inc., April 3, 1996.

33. "Amdahl $145M Deal Gives It More Diversity," *Electronic News*, April 8, 1996; "Facts About Trecom," *Amdahl Update*, April 9, 1996, p. 3.

34. "Facts About Trecom," p. 3; Andrew Jinks, "Everyone, It Seems, Wants To Be An Integrator," *Washington Technology*, April 11, 1996; "Amdahl To Pay $145 Million For Trecom," *Computer Player*, May 1996.

35. "Mergers & Acquisitions," Services Industry Newsletter, May 1996.

36. Casagrande interview, p. 14.

37. Bob Sargenti, interviewed by Kenneth D. Hartsoe, March 26, 1997. Transcript, p. 4.

38. Casagrande interview, p. 15.

39. "Amdahl Acquires Trecom," *The San Francisco Examiner*, April 4, 1996; "Amdahl To Pay $140 Million For Trecom."

40. "Update Answers Your Questions about the Recent TRECOM Announcement," *Amdahl Update*, April 9, 1996, p. 3.

41. "Facts About Trecom," p. 3.

42. "Update Answers Your Questions," p. 2.

43. Doug Henschen, "Marketer, Systems Integrator Ally," *D M News*, July 22, 1996.

44. "Mergers & Acquisitions."

45. Sargenti interview, p. 12.

46. "Update Answers Your Questions," p. 2; Sargenti interview, p. 7.

47. "Update Answers Your Questions," p. 3; "Amdahl Snaps Up Trecom Inc.," *Computing Canada*, April 25, 1996.

48. Charles Enman, "DMR's New Millennium," *Telegraph Journal* (Canada), December 4, 1996; Larry Barrett, "Amdahl Shifts to Service as the Millennium Nears," *Silicon Valley Business Journal*, June 10, 1996.

49. Sargenti interview, p. 13.

50. News Release, April 22, 1997, DMR Consulting Group, Montreal, Quebec, Canada; John Morrissy, "DMR Operations Are Up, Up and Away," *Telegraph Journal*, December 3, 1996.

51. Fonner interview, p. 14.

52. 1996 Annual Report, p. 1.

53. Bill Richards, "Amdahl Says Loss For Second Period To Top Estimates," *Wall Street Journal*, July 16, 1996.

54. 1996 Annual Report.

55. News Release, July 30, 1996; Michael Goldberg, "Amdahl Sees $250M Loss With Change in Direction," *Computerworld*, July 22, 1996.

56. Lewis interview, p. 3.

Chapter Twelve

1. Wright interview, p. 4.

2. Lewis interview, pp. 12–13.

3. Kenneth Flamm, *Creating The Computer*, (Washington D.C: The Brookings Institution, 1988) p. 173.

4. Flamm, *Creating the Computer*, p. 173.

5. Michael G. Borrus, *Competing For Control* (Cambridge, MA: Ballinger Publishing Company, 1988) p. 99.

6. Charles H. Ferguson and Charles R. Morris, *Computer Wars* (New York, NY: Times Books, 1993) p. 224.

7. Takuma Yamamoto, pp. 31–33.

8. Ibid.

9. Flamm, *Creating the Computer*, p. 129.

10. Ibid., pp. 127, 130.

11. Ibid.

12. Yamamoto, p. 57.

13. Ibid., pp. 51, 60, 63–65, 86–87.

14. Flamm, *Creating the Computer*, pp. 180–181.

15. Fujitsu Limited's FY 1998 Financial Results Press release, May 25, 1999.

16. Lewis interview, pp. 9–10.

17. Wright interview, p. 4.

18. Martin Garvey, "Amdahl's CMOS Reaches 80 MIPS – IBM's mainframe processors to hit 90 MIPS," *InformationWeek*, February 9, 1998.

19. 1998 corporate brochure, "Building the Computing Center of the Future," p. 1.

20. Wright interview, p. 1.

21. 1998 corporate brochure, "Building the Computing Center of the Future," p. 3.

22. Wright interview, pp. 1-2.

INDEX

All page numbers in *italics* indicate the inclusion of a photograph or illustration.

211 series Time Division Multiplexer, 67
305 RAMAC computer
    development, 12
    disk memory storage, *14*
    disk use, 13
470V/6 machine, 19 24, 27, *32, 66*
    chips, *34*
    expanded product line, 47, 52
    first sales, 34–37
    initial marketing strategy, 33
    introduction, 31
    price reduction, 47
    testing, 33
    upgradable in the field, 52
    vs. the IBM 370/168, 33, 35
470/7A computer, 57
580 series, 59, *61, 64, 66*
    diversity of products, 67, 70, 71
    features, 60
    investment in, 62
    launch, 61–63
    performance, 59
    problems with, 63–65
    recovery from reliability problems,
        65–67
4705 Communications Processor, 67–68
4705E Communications Processor,
    67–68
4705 Programmable Communications
    Processor, 56, 57
4725 series, 85
4745 Communications Processor, 99
5840, 70
5860 single processor, 59–60
5870 model, 60
5880 multi-processor, 59
5890 series, *74*
    development, 78
    first shipment, 77, 79
    introduction, 77–78
    multiple models, 83
    popularity, 75
5990 series, *82*
    -350 uniprocessor, 89
    -500 entry-level dual processor, 89
    -1100 three-way multiprocessor, 89
    computing capacity, 87
    expansion of line, 89–90
    power, 87
    pricing, 87–88
    revolutionary aspect, 87
5995-1267M, 109
5995 series mainframes
    announcement of, 94
    power, 95
    product line, 95–96
    speed, 95
6000 series, 67
6100 storage processor, 88
6380J disk storage drive, 88
6380K disk storage drive, 88

6380 Storage System, 80
6390 Direct Access Storage Device,
    99–100
6680 Electronic Direct Access Storage,
    77, 80
74655, 97

A

Adaptec, 62–63
Adler, John, 62
Aeronautics, 15
Alexander, Mike, 39
AMDAC. *See* Amdahl Diagnostic
    Assistance Center
Amdahl, Gene, *11, 22, 53*
    360 series, development of, at IBM,
        14–16
Amdahl's Law (*see* Amdahl's Law)
    birthplace, 15
    brilliance, 22
    CEO, steps down as, 54
    CEO duties, sharing with Gene
        White, 53
    confidence, 25
    cycle time, goal for faster, 21
    financing, quest for, 24, 27
    first impressions of the man, 21
    Ford Motor Company, joins, 15
    founds Amdahl Corporation (*see*
        Amdahl Corporation)
    IBM, convincing users to switch from,
        26
    IBM, departs, 13, 15
    IBM, recruitment by, 12, 15
    IBM, returns to, 1960, 15
    Ikeda, meeting with, 130
    Michelson/Morley award, recipient
        of, 47
    Norwegian deal, clinches, 45
    Quissell, Marian D., marriage to, 15
    radical vision for 580 series, 64
    Stanford, teaching position, 15
    strategy when starting compnay, 19
    World War II service, 15
Amdahl, Limited, Canada, 45, 48
Amdahl A.G., 48
Amdahl Capital Corporation, 44
Amdahl Corporation
    1975, first revenues, 39
    acquisitions spur growth,
        122–123
    billion-dollar mark, reaches, 87
    difficult installations, innovative
        solutions to, 43–44
    diversifying product line, *58*
    DMR Group acquisition (*see* DMR
        Group, Inc.)
    earthquake of 1989, helping hand
        during, 90
    employee growth, 51–52, 57, 71

employee petition in support of Gene
    Amdahl, 28
expansion into Pacific Basin, 70, 100
expansion of facilities/production,
    25–26, *40*, 45
favorable press, 54, 57
financial difficulties, early 1990s, 99,
    101
financial returns, 1977, 48
financial struggles, 30–31
financing plan at outset, 19
founding, 19–20
hiring difficulties, as startup, 22
informal atmosphere, 22
initial public offering, 44–45
Kern Avenue facility, 21
Key Computer Laboratories, acquires,
    89
mainframe market, share in, 88
mainframes, marketed as servers,
    104
"million dollar coffee mug" myth, 42
momentum building after first sales,
    43–44
new headquarters, 1978 completion,
    50
patents, 31
personnel cuts, 27, 71, 91, 101, 103
prestige, 47
pricing wars with IBM, 91, 100
profit, first, 1976, 46
profits, falling, 103
public offering, attempts at, 26, 28
recruitment of talent, 46
reorganization, 105–107
repeat customers, 48–49
revenues, 1987, 83
revenues, 1990, 83
rivalry with IBM becomes global,
    45–46
staff doubles, 47
stock value, 63, 100, 103
switch to virtual memory product,
    26–27
twentieth anniversary, 109–110
writedown of mainframe inventories,
    110
Amdahl Deutschland GmbH, 45
Amdahl Diagnostic Assistance Center,
    35, 39
Amdahl France S.A.R.L., 48
Amdahl Global Solutions Group, 81
Amdahl International, 45
Amdahl International Management
    Services, Limited, 81
Amdahl Norge a/s Norway, 45
Amdahl Phenomenon, 69–70
Amdahl's Law, 13, 15–16
Amdahl South Africa, 85
Amdahl Systems Group, 123
Amdahl Television Network, 92

Analytical Machine, 11
Anderson, David L., 93
Anderson Consulting, 114
Annex Research, 106
Antares Alliance Group
        founding, 104
        third generation of ObjectStar, 109
        upper management, 104–105
Apache mainframe, 75, 77. *See also*
        890 series
Armstrong, Bob, 28
Arturi, Manny, 119–*121*
AT&T, *55*, 69
AT&T Canada, 121
Auclair, Michael, 115–116
Australian National Computer Center, 70
Automatic Tabulating Company, 11
AXA Insurance, 121

B

Babbage, Charles, 11
Bartels, Robert, 37, 39
BDM International, Inc., 116
Beebe, Bruce O., 27, 75, 80
Bell, Alan, 46, 81
Bell Labs, 60
Berkeley Computers, 19, 21
Big Three automakers, sales to, 48
Blackwell, Dave, 39
Boucher, Larry, 62
Brewer, Dave, 21–23, 27, 64, 65, 75
BSG. *See* Business Solutions Group
Buckingham Research Group, 108
Building M3, 47
Building M4, 51
Building O-5, 51
Building O-6, 51
Building O-7, 51
Burke, Tom, *121*
Businessland, 113
Business Solutions Group, 108, 113,
        115–116, 134

C

Cardinal, Ed, 27
Caroli, Bill, 85
Casagrande, Frank, 119, *121*
Case Institute of Technology, 47
Cassel, Henry, 22, 70
Cavalier, John, 104–105
Chambers, Dave, 64, 78
chip carrier, *19*
Chuba, Mike, 80
Clements, Mike, 64
CMOS technology. *See* complementary
        metal-oxide semiconductor
        technology
COBOL conversion tools, 105
Coggins, Steve, 45
Columbia, Maryland, field office, 51
Communications Systems Division, 61,
        67, 85
Compata, 16–17
Compatible Systems group, 105

complementary metal-oxide
        semiconductor technology, 85, 107
Computer Decisions, 33
Computer Usage Company, 39
Computerworld, 39
Control Data Corporation, 20
customer confidence, 100
customer satisfaction, 96
Customer Services Group, 105

D

Datamation, 55, 61
Dataquest, 97
data storage product line, 88
DeMory, Tony, 64, 108
Denver, Colorado, field office, 51
Difference Machine, 11
Djurdjevic, Bob, 91, 106
DMR Group, Inc., 111
        acquisition, 110–111
        bidding war for, 115–118
        client base, 114, 121
        corporate culture, 116, 118
        e-business consulting, 135
        employees, 114
        founders, 113–115
        Gartner Group rating, 115
        Olympic scoring system,
        management of, 114
        origins, 113–114
        revenues, 114
        smoothing cultural differences after
        merger, 118–119
Dogmersfield Park Estate, 76, 80–81
Dublin, Ireland, plant, 48–*49*, 53, 57,
        67, 76–77, 107
Ducros, Pierre, 113, 115–116, 118
Dutton, James, 33, 37

E

ECL. *See* emitter-coupled logic
EDAS. *See* 6680 Electronic Direct Access
        Storage
EDS Canada, 114
education, company commitment to,
        68–69
Electronic Data Systems Corporation,
        104
Electronic Numerical Integrator and
        Calculator, 11–*14*
Electrotechnical Laboratory, 128
Ellison, Lawrence J., 22
"Elvis" system. *See* LVS 4500 storage
        system
emitter-coupled logic, 107
Employer of the Year, 1979, 54
ENIAC. *See* Electronic Numerical
        Integrator and Calculator
Enterprise Computing Group, 106,
        111
Enterprise Storage Systems, 105
European Commission, 71
European economy, effects Amdahl's
        sales, 99

European expansion, 48
Extended Architecture, 70

F

FACOM 100, 128
FACOM 230, 129
FACOM 270, 129
Fairchild Camera & Instrument
        Company, 29
Fairchild Semiconductor, 22
Ferone, William, 41, 65, 93, 94
Financial World, 62
Flanagan, Bill, 22, 37
Fonner, Chuck, 122
FONTAC project, 129
Forbes, 83
Fortune magazine, 45
Francesconi, Joseph J., 21, 37, 62, 80,
        93
"FUD" strategy, 41–42
Fujitsu, Ltd., 20–21
        5890 series development, 79
        5990 series development, 88
        Amdahl International, joint venture,
        45
        annual sales, 1999, 131
        computers, research on, 127–131
        computer sales, 1970s, 130
        deeper investment in Amdahl
        Corporation, 24–25, 30
        digital calculator, introduction of
        first, 127
        European resistance to buying
        products from Japan, 48
        founding, 24, 126–127
        IBM compatibility, recognizing
        importance of, 129
        increase in holdings, 71
        integrated circuits, production of,
        129
        joint development deal with Amdahl
        Corporation, 23
        loan to Amdahl, 1993, 107
        mainframe, Japan's first, 129
        maintenance agreements for Amdahl,
        36
        memory chip market, 130
        merger with Amdahl, 125
        name, meaning of, 126–127
        Open Systems Group, 24
        personnel sent to Sunnydale, 24
        rumors of Amdahl buyout, 93
        SPARC chip, 96
        STC merger, discomfort with, 56
        telephone switching systems,
        expertise in, 127
        World War II, impact of, 127

G

Gartner Group, 80, 115
gate design, 22
Gemini Computers, 19, 21
General Electric, 22, 29
General Motors Corporation, 104

Gonzalez, Fred, 42–43
GOSIP. *See* Government Open Systems Interconnection Protocol
Government Open Systems Interconnection Protocol, *97*
Governor's Committee for Employment of the Handicapped, 54
Great Lakes Research and Development, 99
Grodhaus, Greg, 109

H

Handschuh, Greg, 72
Harvard Business Review, 54–55
Heizer, E.F., Jr., 20–21, 29, 71
Heizer Corporation, 19–20, 71
Henry VIII, 81
"Hickory" systems, 59
Hitachi Data Systems, 93
Hollerith, Herman, *10*–11
Hollerith Tabulating Machine, *10*
Honeywell Information Systems, 29
Hourihan, Dick, *121*
"H" systems, 59
Huron system
    Antares Alliance Group, relationship with, 105
    development, 97–98
    introduction, 97
    market impact, lack of, 99
    ObjectStar, name change to, 105
    popularity, 98–99
    sales force, transition for, 98
Hydro Quebec, 70

I

IBM. *See* International Business Machines
IBM Canada, 114
IBM Canada, Limited, 116–117
IBM Principles of Operations Manual, 71
Ikeda, Toshio, 23, 127–129
InCASE data modeling, 105
InformationWEEK, 83
initial public offering, Amdahl, 44–45
Inland Revenue, 99
Intel, 22
International Business Machines, 11
    360 series, *11*, 14, 16
    370, 26
    370/158, *44*
    370/168, 33
    370/195, 36
    370 Model 145 computer, 22–23
    390 System, 107, 111, 133
    650, 13
    3033, 70
    3081 processor, 59
    3090 System, 83
    aggressiveness toward Amdahl Corporation, 62, 91
    antitrust suit, 57, 62

domination of marketplace, 26
    "fear, uncertainty, and doubt," fights back with, 41–42
    Los Gatos facility, 15
    pricing, 16, 72, 79, 91, 100
    profits, dropping, early 1990s, 99
    transistor assembly line, 14
IT Services and Support, 134

J

Japan vs. U.S. trade dispute, 84
John Hancock Financial, 114

K

Katharine of Aragon, 81
Key Computer Laboratories, 89
Knudsen, Helge, 98

L

Labe, Peter, 108–109
large-scale integrated circuitry, 22
Larsen, Reed W., 22, 25
LeClair, Ed, 67
Lewis, Jack, 53, 55, 57, 60, 67, 69, 73, 83
    on Amdahl's strategy, 79–80
    "architect," Amdahl as, 107
    background, 47–48
    CEO, named as, 61
    chairman of the board, named, 85
    Dogmersfield Park Estate, opening of, 81
    elected to board of directors, 48
    Fujitsu, Ltd., merger with Amdahl, role in, 125
    Huron system, sees opportunity in, 98
    joins Amdahl Corporation, 48
    retirement, 125–126
    structure to company, adds, 48
    Zemke retirement, steps in after, 119
    Zemke's promotion, comments on, 101
Los Angeles Olympics, 114
Los Gatos Development Lab, 62
LSI. *See* large-scale integrated circuitry
Lutalah, John, 118
LVS 4500 storage system, 109, 122
LVS 4600, 133

M

macrocode, development of, 59–60
Madden, Clifford J., 54
Magnuson, 73
Maier, Robert, 28
mainframes, decline in use, 103
Malone, Michael, 17
Manufacturer's Life, Canada, 46
Mark I, 11, *12*
MASCOR. *See* Multiple Access Systems Corporation
Massachusetts Mutual Life Insurance Company, 39

Matthews, John, 42, 65
Mauchly, John, 11
McIntyre, Wayne, 43
Meilleur, Serge, 113, 119
Memorex Corporation, 55
Merger Management Review, 119
Michelson/Morley award, 47
Microsoft, 114, 135
Middlesex, England, offices, 48
Miles, Eric L., 93
Millennium 700 series, 133
Millennium 830, *131*
Millennium CMOS mainframe, 131–132
Millennium software, 109
Miner, Robert, 22
Ministry of International Trade and Industry, 128
M&M Mars, 121
Mondex Global Electronic Cash Program, 122
Montreal Summer Olympic Games, 114
Moscow Olympics, 114
Motorola Semiconductor Products and Advanced Memory System, Inc., 22
Multiple Access Systems Corporation, 19, 21
Multiple Domain Feature, 60, 89
Multiple Virtual Storage Systems Extensions Assist software, 52
MVS/370, 70
MVS/SEA. *See* Multiple Virtual Storage Systems Extensions Assist software
MVS/XA, 70
MVS/XA/Conversion Assist Feature, 70

N

NASA Goddard Institute for Space Studies, 34, 36, 37, 39
National Advanced Systems, 73, 79
National Bank of Canada, 121
National Semiconductor, 84, 93
NEC, 130
NET. *See* Network Equipment Technologies
Network Equipment Technologies, 21, 93
Nixdorf, Heinz, 24
Nixdorf Computer, 24–25
Nutt, Ollie J., 43, 108

O

Oates, Edward, 22
ObjectStar, 105, 111, 122
O'Connell, Bill, 41, 80, 98
Okada, Kanjiro, 127
O'Neill, Bert, 24, 71
Ontario Teachers Pension Board, 116
Open Enterprise Systems, 105
Operating Council, 123
Oracle Corporation, 61, 77
Oracle Systems Corporation, 22
Oregon Department of Transportation, 114
OS/390 mainframes, 133

PQ

Peripheral Products Division, 60, 85
Philips' Gloeilampenfabrieken, 48
Pigeon, Jacques, 117
Plonka, Gene, 44
plug-compatible mainframe computers, 57
Poehner, Michael J., 113, 115, 118
Poughkeepsie, New York, IBM plant, 14–15
Powell, Russ, *121*
Pozos, Anthony, 80, 91
Pratt, Charlie, 36
Price Pritchett, 119
pricing wars with IBM, 91, 100
prime number, largest, discovery of, 90
Prince Charles, 81
Princess Anne, 81
Pritchett and Associates, Inc., 118–119

Qantas Airways, 114
Quebec, Province of, 121
Quissell, Marian D., 15

RST

RAID. *See* redundant arrays of independent disks
Ramo Woolridge, 15
RCA, 22
Reagan administration, 84
redundant arrays of independent disks, 109
Relational Technology, Inc., 61
Reliability Plus, rating of 6380, 67
Reliability Research, Inc., rating of Model 5890-300, 83
Roy, Alain, 113, 116
RW440 process control computer, 15
Ryan, Bruce, 115

Sargenti, Robert, 120
Scalable Processor Architecture, 96
Sears Roebuck, 114
Securities and Exchange Commission, 26, 28, 44
Shahbazian, Mike, 103–104
Shattuck, Harold O., 19
Silicon Valley, 15, 17, 22, 26, 90
Simonds, Ken, 35, 62
SmartCard Group, 122
Software Pursuits, 67
Solid Logic Technology, 16
Southern Company, 133
SPARC. *See* Scalable Processor Architecture
Spectric storage system, 109
Spectris Platinum RAID-1 system, 133

SRAM. *See* Static Random Access Memory chip
St. Louis, Missouri, field office, 51
Stanford University, 15
Static Random Access Memory chip, 99
Storage Technology Corporation, 55–56
Sun Microsystems, Inc., 96, 106
Sunnyvale, *18*, 24, 25, 39, 45, 47, 76, 130
Swiss Railways, 45
Swords, Ireland plant. *See* Dublin, Ireland, plant
Systems Network Architecture, IBM, 68

Taylor, Mike, 93
*team*server, 133
Telefunken Computers, 24
Texas Instruments, 22
The Big Score, 17
Thompson, Edward F., 44, 69, 100
Thompson, Ernest B., 51
Tierney, Daniel W., 62
Topham, Lyle, 19, 21, 108
Tran Telecommunications, 53, 56, 86
TRECOM Business Systems, Inc.
    acquisition by Amdahl, 120
    overview, 119
    revenues, 120
    strengths, 120–121
    Year-2000 software conversions, 121
Trilogy Systems, 55, 69

UVW

United States Censuc Bureau, 11
United States Fidelity and Guaranty, 109
United States Postal Service, 69
University of Alberta, 39
University of Michigan Computing Center, 37, 39
Unix, 60, 100
Unix Systems, 94
Urano, Mr., 71
U.S. vs. Japan trade dispute. *See* Japan vs. U.S. trade dispute
UTS 2.1, 94, 97
UTS/580, 77, 80
UTS/580 Release 1.2, 85
UTS software
    disappointing sales, 94
UTS system, 60, 77

Valid Logic Systems, 89
Virtual Machine/Performance Enhancement software, 53
virtual memory, 21, 26
VM/PE. *See* Virtual Machine/ Performance Enhancement software

Watson, Thomas J., 11
Western Electric, 45
White, Eugene, *28*, *37*, 44, *47*, 53, 55, 57, 65
    Antares Alliance Group, appointment to, 104
    background, 29
    consultancy to Amdahl Corporation, 29–30
    increasing Amdahl Corporation's efficiency, 31
    joins company, 29
    presidency, 30–31
    steps down as CEO, 61, 69
    vice chairman of the board, named, 85
Williams, Peter V., 41, 46, 81
Williams, Raymond A., 19, 33
WISC. *See* Wisconsin Integrally Synchronized Computer
Wisconsin Integrally Synchronized Computer, 15
Woman's Network, 54
World Business Weekly, 51
Wright, David
    Amdahl Systems Group, promotion to, 123
    background, 106
    CEO, promotion to, 125
    challenges at time of Fujitsu merger, 131–132
    joins Amdahl, 107
    on core competencies, 135
    restructuring, 134
    "synergies," 132
    total strategy, 134

XYZ

Xerox Business Systems, 48

Yamamoto, Takuma, 130
Yoshioka, Yoshiro, 24

Zasio, John, 22
Zemke, E. Joseph
    on the 5890 series, 78–79
    background, 75
    CEO, promotion to, 101
    comments on 1991 revenue decline, 100–101
    Huron system, sees opportunity in, 98
    joins Amdahl Corporation, 75, 76
    management realignment, position on, 93–94
    president, named, 85
    retirement, 119
Zenith Data Systems, 113